Imprint:

© 2015 by Miriam Goodspeed / Ingrid Vallières
Graphic Illustration: Karl-Heinz Bruder, Krefeld
Composition: Angelika Fleckenstein; spotsrock.de

ISBN: 978-3-7323-5909-7 (Paperback)
       978-3-7323-5910-3 (Hardcover)
       978-3-7323-5911-0 (e-Book)

Verlag tredition GmbH Hamburg

The work, including its parts is copyright protected. Any use is prohibited without the consent of the publisher and the author. This is especially true for electronic or other copying, translation, dissemination and public disclosure.

Miriam Goodspeed / Ingrid Vallières

Mirrors Within Mirrors

Unforgettable Adventures Into Past Lives
shared by Reincarnation Therapist Ingrid Vallieres
ImWritten by Miriam Goodspeed

Miriam Goodspeed,

an award winning writer and actress with credits in both journalism and scriptwriting, has appeared in over 11 major and independent movies. She is fascinated by the idea that "we have lived before." and remembered several of her own in past life sessions conducted by Ms. Vallieres.

Ingrid Vallieres

Since her childhood she knew that there had to be more than one lifetime. Being adventurous and curious she explored different schools of thought early on in her life. In her personal path she has relived her own past lives and studied the subject to become a past life therapist - long before there was such a profession in the public field.

During her career, Ingrid Vallieres has worked as a translator, psychologist, book author, lecturer and trainer. She is an instructor in counselling psychology and regression therapy and conducts in-house corporate seminars.

I have known Ingrid Vallieres for over 20 years and admire her for her work and what she has accomplished in her life. Her own story and the case regression histories of some of her many clients is a fascinating tale about an adventurous woman who pioneered in the study of past life therapy. She continues to aid others to move on in this life by solving lingering problems from past lives. Through her work she has shown that life does not end in nothingness but goes on forever.

Table of contents

Chapter-by-Chapter Outline 9

CHAPTER 1 - "WE HAVE ALWAYS EXISTED" 19

CHAPTER 2 - YES, OF COURSE WE CAN REMEMBER 22

CHAPTER 3 - SEARCHING FOR TRUTHS IN ALL THE RIGHT PLACES 38

CHAPTER 4 - ANSWERS MAY LIE IN MYSTICAL INDIA 47

CHAPTER 5 - THOSE FARAWAY PLACES 59

CHAPTER 6 - HER GEISHA PAST IS CALLING 63

CHAPTER 7 - ENLIGHTEN ME, ASIA! 71

CHAPTER 8 - THE GERMAN GEISHA 76

CHAPTER 9 - LOVE AND TRAGEDY 82

CHAPTER 10 - THE PATH BECOMES CLEAR 88

CHAPTER 11 - THE ANSWERS LIE IN OUR PAST 91

CHAPTER 12 - PIONEERING IN PAST LIFE THERAPY 96

CHAPTER 13 - KARMA LINKS 101

CHAPTER 14 - PRENATAL AND BIRTH EXPERIENCES 105

CHAPTER 15 - WHAT ABOUT TWINS? 110

CHAPTER 16 - UNCOUNTABLE LIFETIMES 114

CHAPTER 17 - MANY APPROACHES TO REGRESSION 119

CHAPTER 18 - SELF INDUCING YOUR OWN REGRESSION 126

CHAPTER 19 - GINA WAS INTRIGUING 132

CHAPTER 20 - RESOLVING THOSE "FATAL FLAWS" 148

CHAPTER 21 - MARGO AND DIETER WERE SOUL MATES 152

CHAPTER 22 - ERIC AND KATJA 159

CHAPTER 23 - GARY'S STORY 166

CHAPTER 24 - WE ARE THE SUM OF ALL OUR LIVES 171

CHAPTER 25 - BEAUTY ISN'T EVERYTHING 176

CHAPTER 26 - REGRESSION BEGINS 180

CHAPTER 27 - INGRID REMEMBERS PAST LIVES 188

CHAPTER 28 - NEW UNDERSTANDINGS 194

SUPPLEMENT 200

Chapter-by-Chapter Outline

Chapter 1
"We Have Always Existed"

Ingrid Vallieres, a tall, beautiful blonde with bright blue eyes, is considered to be a pioneer in Germany's large community of past life therapists. Born Ingrid Kreuzwieser in Stuttgart, Germany in 1953, she is a woman who has practiced and taught her craft not only in her own country but throughout Europe, Asia and in the United States. Her philosophy is a simple one: perhaps we have always existed - in one way or another - since the beginning of time.

Chapter 2
Yes, Of Course We Can Remember

In revealing Ingrid's early life and her youthful search for the meaning behind life, we discover how throughout her childhood, she has memory flashes of past lives. Early on, she realizes she has an unusual gift for languages. Somehow, she is able to pick up languages so well that those speaking the languages as their mother tongue would hardly notice her slight accent. She learns the Oriental martial arts and becomes fascinated with Asian cultures. Later she will discover in reincarnation regressions that she lived many past lives in the Near and Far East as well as in the Western World.

Chapter 3
Searching For Truths In All The Right Places

Ingrid and her new best friend Roland set out to search for the true meaning of life. At one point, they visit a Yoga school in the Black Forest for a two week stay. There, Ingrid makes her decision to become a vegetarian like the Swami and his followers. When she is asked to translate a visiting Sikh master's lectures from English to German, she finds him fascinating. And when he invites her to visit him in India, she promises she will do so. It would be a promise she will keep when she turned 17.

Chapter 4
Answers May Lie in Mystical India

When she graduates from school at 17, Ingrid talks her parents into letting her go to India. While she supposedly is traveling with her good friend and fellow truth seeker Roland, when they arrive in India she leaves him in Bombay to meditate while she travels around the country by herself.

This chapter deals with her six week visit and the adventures and glimpses of past lives she finds during her travels. Here, she discovers that the Sikh she had promised to visit is the wrong guru for her. She then finds her true spiritual leader.

Chapter 5
Those Faraway Places

Two years later, at 19, she again travels to Asia, this time alone. She finds adventure and a new love in Bangkok before realizing that her destiny lies elsewhere. She goes on to visit Japan.

Chapter 6
Her Geisha Past Is Calling

Japan is a hauntingly familiar place to her. She was never here before in her life, so how does she know so much about it? She begins to remember strange things, as if she had lived here in a past life. She has a number of unusual encounters in Japan, including reoccurring memories as both a high born Geisha and as a Samurai warrior. At The Conservative University of the Martial Arts in Tokyo she is welcomed and given a Kendo uniform, the headgear, gloves and wooden sword. Later she leaves Tokyo to visit the temples of Kyoto where she has further visions of her past lives in that country.

Chapter 7
Enlighten Me, Asia!

Ingrid leaves Japan briefly to visit Korea. While there, she visits the Tae Kwon Do Association headquarters. Returning to Japan, she realizes that, although her vacation is nearing its end, she doesn't want to leave Japan. She sends a message to her German company that she is quitting her job.

Chapter 8
The German Geisha

Back in Tokyo, she finds temporary living quarters and hunts for work. Soon she has a job as a translator. Then a friend introduces her into a new world, that of a hostess in a Japanese nightclub. She moves to an even more exclusive club. Soon, she is also modeling fashions and doing photo shoots for magazines. To her delight, Ingrid is now earning five times her previous German salary in these new jobs.

Chapter 9
Love and Tragedy

Ingrid becomes engaged to a Japanese man. Life is perfect until tragedy strikes when a stove explodes in her face. Burned over 43 percent of her body, she has a Near Death experience in which she leaves her body for a brief time. Hanging between life and death, she is given the choice of staying in this world or returning to the world between lives. She decides to live in spite of her extreme physical pain. It wasn't her time to die and she knows she had a mission to fulfill. Ingrid returns to Germany, not knowing what lies ahead of her.

Chapter 10
The Path Becomes Clear

From her near death experience, Ingrid has learned a great life's secret – bad experiences can help us in the end, if we look at them in a positive life. Something better was coming. As she recuperates from her injuries, her friend Roland tells her of how he just had a past life regression and suggests she should look into this new philosophy, too. Roland leads her to find her life's purpose.

Chapter 11
The Answers Lie In Our Past.

Suffering from depression, melancholy and lack of self esteem after her accident and the death of all her great plans in Japan, Ingrid now seeks ways to recover her inner stability. She wonders if the answers might lie in her past lives. She first studies Dianetics for several years, and marries a new love Marc Vallieres. Although Marc is deeply into the movement, Ingrid wants to move on. Marc and she have an amiable separation and divorce.

In the mid 1970's, Ingrid goes to California to study with Dr. Morris Netherton, an authority in the field of past life regression.

She returns to Germany in 1978 to find that reincarnation is becoming a hot topic thanks to a book by a German author, Thorwald Dethlefsen.

Chapter 12
Pioneering In Past Life Therapy

Home once again in Stuttgart, Ingrid still has no idea what will happen next in her life. Looking upon her reincarnation studies as a hobby, she forms a translation company. Friends beg her to regress them. At first she does it for free until her client list in this grows so large she decides to begin charging for her work. She forms a new company, The Institute for Past Life Research.

Her spiritual path suddenly becomes a practical profession. It astounds her more than anyone else. Her new clients come to her as unbelievers and, as their past lifetimes are laid out for them, become believers.

Chapter 13
Karmic Links

In this chapter, Ingrid explains karmic links between souls, in which people are reincarnated in the same "casts" of friends and relatives over and over again. Ingrid's studies indicate that we pick our parents and the lives we lead in order to learn certain lessons in live. She gives the reader several exercises to do in this chapter.

Chapter 14
Prenatal and Birth Experiences

Ingrid explains that the basis of all past life work is the prenatal and birth experience. Everything that happens in pregnancy, even the music the mother plays, is picked up and stored by the baby growing within her body. The soul's hunger for life is so strong that it will even push a couple together in order to be born even in unfortunate circumstances. Acceptance by parents of the upcoming birth is important. The first time the mother realizes she is pregnant is the first greeting given her baby, and that baby will take it in and store it in its subconscious. The way we react to the trauma of birth establishes how we handle stress in our later life.

Chapter 15
What About Twins?

In this chapter, we study how twins are separate souls, yet their lives are often entwined for better or for worse. Sometimes twins were rivals in past lives, such as Kristine and Sylvia. Both women uncover identical stories about their pasts and are stunned to learn that the other had experienced them, too. Helmut always hated his twin for good reason. They were old enemies, and the brother was their parents' favorite in this lifetime. Also explored is the moment of conception, how we choose our parents and how important it is to us if our mothers accept us without any thought of rejection.

Chapter 16
Uncountable Lifetimes

Here, Ingrid discusses some of her regressions, including overcoming her own fear of spiders. She explains that in regression work, fears are handled by directly addressing them. Many of our irrational fears and minor illnesses, such as headaches, can be explained by events from our past lives.

Chapter 17
Many Approaches to Regression

In this chapter, Ingrid outlines in depth the various approaches to regression work. These include psychic readings, symbolic therapy, problem and non problem oriented therapy, hypnosis and the non hypnotic approach. She explains why she prefers the latter.

Chapter 18
Self Inducing Your Own Regression

Ingrid offers a few simple ways for anyone to experience one of their own regressions. Ingrid notes, however, that no therapy can be done through do-it-yourself regressions, as you need an experienced therapist to help you through it.

Chapter 19
Gina Was Intriguing

This chapter deals with one of Ingrid Vallieres most exciting cases. It points out that we may have all existed - in one way or another - since the beginning of time. Learning the truth about our past lives will resolve any problem and bring us relief in this, our present life. It goes into depth on the various past lives of "Gina", a German woman who once danced the "dance of love" as a young priestess in a temple dedicated to Kore, daughter of Demeter.

Chapter 20
Resolving Those Fatal Flaws

As shown in the past lives of Ingrid's clients, you can be freed of your past "fatal flaws." In every lifetime, there is a turning point where we can change everything, but such a decision can carry a terrible price. If we fail to accomplish what we were sent here to accomplish, life can get very difficult in the births that follow. We can, through past life therapy, learn from this mistake, clean it up and change our ways.

Chapter 21
Margo and Dieter Were Soul Mates

Margo and Dieter, husband and wife, had been together for many lifetimes. He had also experienced a lifetime as a space alien. An artist in this lifetime, in many of his pictures he keeps drawing the face of an unknown woman. One day, he meets her. She is Magda. Both are regressed by Ingrid with surprising results.

Chapter 22
Eric and Katja

As did Dieter in the previous story, Eric also has a dream girl, Katja, but the two souls never seem to get together, whether it's in this lifetime or in the many previous ones they have shared. He also remembers a humiliating experience in one lifetime in connection with an Egyptian queen. Ingrid helps him solve his problems.

Chapter 23
Gary's Story

Gary was a Roman ruler who fell in love with an Egyptian queen. They want to combine their countries, but Rome refuses to consider it. He is killed when he returns to Rome. In this life, Gary regrets subconsciously not being able to handle this past life more successfully.

Chapter 24
We Are the Sum of All Our Lives

How we each have a higher consciousness which is always present, especially after death, and how we need to learn to live simultaneously at all levels of consciousness. Our subconscious will put up blocks to prevent an incident from a past life to reoccur in this one.

In this chapter, we learn of Renata who continued to "blow it" over and over again until she learned "why".

Chapter 25
Beauty Isn't Everything

Beauty isn't everything, Ingrid tells us as she discusses one of her clients. Renata is a beautiful woman, who came to her because just as everything was going well they seemed to go bad. As Ingrid points out, for every recurring problem, there is a fully fledged past life at the cause, and so there was for Renata. In this chapter we also learn the story of Bridget and her sons and how their past lives were now affecting their present ones.

Chapter 26
Regression Begins

Ingrid explains how she begins each course of reincarnation therapy with a preliminary talk. From this she obtains a picture of your life situation. Important points are the experiences of childhood and your relationship with your parents and siblings. The nature of these interactions reflects past roles. Everything you encounter continuously in this life and find hard to bear are signs of past experiences which haven't been pleasant. The beginnings and endings of life do not always come easily. This chapter is an in depth discussion of her methods.

Chapter 27
Ingrid Remembers Past Lives.

Ingrid explains how over the years, she has been regressed by a number of other people and has regressed herself as well using her own techniques. She tells of some of her past lives in Germany, Japan and Florida in the U.S. She believes she chose her family in this life because in her last one, her best friend became her father in this present life.

Chapter 28
New Undertakings

It has been many years now since Ingrid Vallieres began her journey first into self discovery and then into starting her life's work as one of Germany's pioneer past life therapists. She is the founder of the Institute for Past Life Research and Creative Management International, (CMI) which is a consulting firm in which she offers leadership conferences and other services. She is the author of five books and has a starring role in a European documentary about reincarnation. She continues her lecturing at seminars throughout Europe. The Russians honored her for her work and gave her a professorship. She is happy to say that "Today our story (about reincarnation and past life therapy) is out of the closet and trumpeted around the world.

CHAPTER 1

"WE HAVE ALWAYS EXISTED"

German Past Life therapist Ingrid Vallieres' philosophy is a simple one: perhaps we have always existed - in one form or another - since the beginning of time.

Ingrid, a tall, beautiful blonde with bright blue eyes, is considered to be a pioneer in Germany's large community of past life therapists. "When people tell me emphatically that they don't believe in reincarnation the theory that we return from the state we call death to live again in a new body - I suspect strongly that they really do believe, deep down inside but deny its possibility because of fear," she says.

"You have nothing to fear. Fear is often only a lack of knowledge."

Born Ingrid Kreuzwieser in Stuttgart, Germany in 1953, she is a woman who has practiced and taught her craft not only in her own country but throughout Europe, Asia and the United States. She often hears from her audiences that if reincarnation really does happen to us, it is obvious that God erases those memories of past lives in our present existence. Should we try to learn something against God's wishes?

Ingrid says that "I tell them that this isn't necessarily against those wishes, for otherwise it would be impossible to tap into our pasts. But these truths will liberate us, for if we have something hidden away, it will not rest until we learn the truth. The truth will always resolve the mystery and bring us relief. Hiding from it, denying it, only prolongs our misery in this life."

She maintains that "Yes, it is true. We will live again after this lifetime. You and I have lived many lives before the one we are now experiencing. I know, for I not only remember my own former lives, but I have done thousands of regressions for clients all over the world."

She explains that sometimes, in spite of the barriers to remembering our consecutive lives, shadows of our past can still affect us.

For example, have you ever visited a place for the first time, yet you "knew" you had been there before? Or have you met a stranger and felt an instant rapport or perhaps an intense dislike, this in spite of never having met this person before in your life?

Perhaps you are half remembering that place or those people from a past life experience.

Ingrid Vallieres has heard many speak of such experiences during her years of practicing past life therapy. When she began her work in the late 1970's, she was among the first in Germany to practice in this new field. She also became a lecturer on the subject and offers seminars to those wishing to learn more about reincarnation therapy.

She began her therapy work after years of study and exploration in this field.

Sometimes the people who come to her for regression into their former lives still suffer traumas from their past, when they resided in other lands and experienced far different circumstances from what they have now. Through regression, they often find the peace of mind and understanding they have sought for so long.

Ingrid explains that in the usual first few regressions, lives experienced by her clients over the past few thousand years are revealed.

"Most of us will tap into lifetimes dealing with protecting and aiding personal or group survival in wars, famines, various natural catastrophes and other types of violence," she explains, adding that "the personal conscience is trying to keep those memories submerged. We forget so we can survive."

She goes on to say that "of course, we don't successfully forget our past, we only temporarily suppress it, so we can only forget for a time. But the past remains part of us. It will make itself remembered through fears, allergies, apprehension and other unpleasant symptoms. Every time we have an unusual or extremely strong reaction to a happening, we are echoing experiences in our past."

She believes that because of a rapid explosion of population all over the earth, humanity is in the middle of an acceleration of evolution "The last five thousand years have been very busy ones. Wherever there is violence, loss and death, many symptoms arise, such as fears, discomfort, depression, physical discomfort and destructive behavior. That's why regressions attempt to get into those traumatic roots experienced in our past."

When she gives her lectures, one of the questions often asked her is "How did you ever get started in past life therapy?"

"I suppose I could say it was my destiny," she admits.

CHAPTER 2

YES, OF COURSE WE CAN REMEMBER

Ingrid Vallieres claims to have lived many lifetimes all over the world.

She believes that she was drawn to this work from the very beginning of her current lifetime, although it took a near death experience to propel her into this field.

"I became involved with past life therapy because it is my purpose, the reason I was born into this present lifetime, to go into this field and to deeply explore the layers of the human mind," she says. "Today, I am pleased to say that I am considered one of the pioneers in this work."

Although she initially started her practice in Germany, she has many family ties in the United States. Soon she brought her work to the U. S. as well as to Canada.

She tells her questioners that she truly believes we carry over all memories from other lives we have lived, and all our experiences and past lives.

"Sometimes the veil of forgetfulness is pierced by accident, yet we can also deliberately draw aside those curtains of our past. We can examine those lives, and, by examining them, strengthen this life we now live."

She says that she has often done this, and that anyone else with a real zest to know their past can do the same. When people ask her how it all began, they often remark that they want to learn more about this intriguing idea of past lives. Could they, too, have lived before? She smiles and always says "Certainly."

She has written many books about her work. All are in German. Several have been translated into other languages. Her first book, Reincarnation Therapy was subsequently translated into English to be published by Ashgrove Press in England and a French version published by Editions Mortagne in Montreal, Canada.

Other books written by Ingrid Vallieres include Astrology and Reincarnation, Reincarnation for Cats, Schicksalstherapy translated as Fate Therapy. Probleme? Nein, danke (translated as Problems? No Thanks, a problem solving manual.) The last three books, only available in German, were published by Editions S. Naglschmid in Stuttgart.

Mirrors Within Mirrors, the title of this book, reflects the infinity of human life. Have you ever stood with two large mirrors, one in front of you and one in back? Remember how you are reproduced again and again until your image is so tiny you can't even distinguish it anymore? Rather like looking into infinity, isn't it? So do our past lives stretch into infinity.

But when you regress, those past lives lost in time become clear once more. And if there were pain or unresolved issues from those past lives, these will be finally healed.

Ingrid was her parents' third child and only daughter. She has three brothers, Bernd, who is five years older than she; Gerhard who is two and a half years older; and Dieter, 14 years her junior.

Her grandmother Susan was a German war bride who lost her first husband during World War II. She married Peter, an American G.I. after the end of the war and moved with him to the United States. Ingrid's mother Ellen, who was an only child, was already grown and stayed behind in Germany.

"My Grandmother would send Mother parcels with food and clothing, because only bare necessities for everyday living were available in Germany for a number of years after World War II," she says.

The fact that her grandmother had married an American greatly influenced Ingrid's life. When she was two years old, she and her two older brothers went to the United States with her mother to visit their grandmother and step grandfather who were living in Pennsylvania. They stayed for a year. Ingrid's father had to stay home and work. Ingrid reflects that considering 1955 was still a postwar era in Germany," it was a financial relief to have the whole family taken care of by my grandparents for awhile."

She returned to the United States when she was five years old.

"I remember it vividly. Again, it was by boat. Again, my father remained behind in Germany. Ships and travel have always played a very important part in my life.

"I spent the first grade in Frackville, Pennsylvania, a very enjoyable experience. We had single benches where in Germany two pupils were always seated together. I still have my first report card from there, showing all A's and B's. I was baptized at my grandparents' church that year, and I went to Sunday school every week. I learned to speak English very quickly. It is well known that young children exposed to foreign, new languages can usually learn them very fast, and so it was in my case. For some reason, I have always found it easy to learn new languages and to speak them fluently."

The family was to return to Germany at the end of the children's school year. But only Ingrid and her mother went home.

"My older brothers were allowed to remain behind to be raised by Grandmother. I, too, wanted to stay, and I had a big fight with my parents about it. But they were adamant, and perhaps they wanted to have the pleasure of raising one of their children back in Germany."

Once back home, she discovered a bonus from her year in the States. She was allowed to enter the second grade that fall, which made her a year ahead scholastically of other German youngsters her age and allowed her to complete her studies at sixteen.

"Somehow, even as a child, I always knew that this wasn't my first time on this planet.

To me, the real question has always been the fate of the soul. What happens after our earthly life? Every boundary has two sides to it - our present existence and the other side.

"Although I couldn't express it verbally, when I was two years old I had a very strong feeling that 'this time I'm going to make it,' whatever 'it' was. Even then, I had this great urge to put all my acquired experience and knowledge to work and not to be distracted until I reached my goal. I remember visualizing this goal as that point of no return where I could stay in my inner center and transcend worldly issues. Such strange thoughts for a tiny child!"

Ingrid was eight when she faced the idea of reincarnation for the first time, "although somehow I had known about it all my life," she says.

"You must understand that I was always a religious child who said her prayers and attended church without urging from my parents. I remember that Sunday even now, after all these years. Our minister was delivering a sermon, talking about salvation, heaven and eternal life. I pulled insistently at Mama's sleeve. "Mama," I said, "I've lived a thousand lives. You just don't go to heaven and stay there!"

"How shocked Mama was as she shushed me into silence. But despite her reaction, I knew that what I had blurted out was true.

"Throughout my childhood, time and again I would have flashes of remembering and recognizing landscapes, pictures, sounds and feelings. It would occur to me that I had experienced the same types of problems before, such as feeling cornered, under pressure to do well in school or feeling adventurous. At such times, I felt that no one could stop me."

Ingrid was an incorrigible runaway in her childhood. The first time was at the age of ten in what she calls "one of my more invincible moments." She explains that it was because of difficulties with her then current teacher whom she thought was "autocratic and overbearing." She was wandering along a highway outside of town when the local police spotted her and insisted on driving her home.

"Why on earth, Ingrid!" asked her exasperated mother.

"I'm all grown up inside, Mama," Ingrid protested. "Why can't I leave home and be on my own?"

Needless to say, "Mama" wasn't very sympathetic to her daughter's protestations of adulthood!

That was also the year she and her best friend developed a "secret alphabet." For each German letter, they developed another character and wrote letters to each other in this newly created alphabet. Years later, Ingrid would discover that their "secret alphabet" was identical with the Celtic Runes.

"Perhaps my friend and I had tapped into another lifetime where the Runes had been our way of writing."

Her grandmother and she always had a special empathy for and connection with each other, and the summer she was eleven, Ingrid felt an intense desire to visit her.

"I had spent those several years with her as a young child, so now I prayed intensely for her to invite me back. Sure enough! Although I didn't tell anyone else about my desires, a few months later Grandmother sent me an airplane ticket and an invitation to spend the summer with her.

"Do I believe in prayers being answered? You bet! I've always believed in God, in a force within us and beyond all material appearance."

There were many similarities between her grandmother and herself, she remembers, including the love of animals, a fierce independence and a strong belief in the supernatural. They spent a happy few months together that summer before she returned to Stuttgart and the start of her fall school term.

Ingrid says as a child she was not only independent but also adventurous and seldom if ever asked her family's approval of her plans.

"Born a Capricorn, I was never childish. After all, if you remember, I traveled to the United States by myself at the age of eleven and again at thirteen. Yearning for adulthood and for life to be started, I never accepted 'no' as an answer for anything."

She says her mother was the disciplinarian of the family who showed more emotion over her daughter's various adventures than her father who could be reached by logic.

"Mama always says Papa was soft on me because I was 'the apple of his eye.' Later, when I went into past life regression, I learned that he and I had been best friends when we fought together in World War II. I died in that war and was quickly reincarnated as his child. He always let me do what I wanted, trusting that I'd be the reliable comrade as if he somehow remembered me to be that in our last lives. We had an equal partnership, which was unusual in a German family, I must admit. I could usually count on his help when I needed it."

One such time happened when she was fourteen. Her parents had a rule that on Saturdays, if she came home before 6:00 p.m., she could go out again. That particular Saturday, she came home before six o'clock, but when she prepared to go out later, she was forbidden to go.

"Not tonight, Ingrid," her mother said in a firm voice.

"Why not?" Ingrid demanded. "I came home on time this afternoon."

"Because I said so," she replied, using, as Ingrid says," that awful excuse so often used by parents throughout the ages."

Ingrid stomped up to her room and looked around.

"No, she's not going to get away with it!" she told herself.

She climbed out her window onto a 12 ft. high balcony. From there she had to maneuver past a tree whose branches tore at her as she clambered over the railing and dropped down to the ground. She listened for a moment but heard nothing. Good. No one was aware of her escape!

She scampered off down the road and into the city.

"I must admit that it wasn't all that exciting an adventure," Ingrid remembers ruefully. "I went to the home of a friend and visited with her. Her parents, of course, didn't know I didn't have permission to be there. Finally, around 4:00 a.m., I decided to go home. My dilemma lay in getting back into the house, because I surely couldn't climb back up the way I came down."

Teeth chattering from the cold, Ingrid stood outside the front door hoping that maybe her father would be awake. She didn't know that her mother had discovered her absence shortly after she left home. They later told her they had been up all night worrying about her.

Finally, she got the courage to knock. To her relief, her father opened the door. "Ingrid! Thank God! You're safe," he said as he hugged her.

Her mother was also happy to have her safe at home, but they both were very angry with her over this escapade.

Fortunately for Ingrid, both of her parents were usually more lenient with their young daughter than many other German parents were with their children.

"As Mama says, I usually showed very good sense. I kept up my grades in school and I had a maturity unusual in a person of my age. I would have left home at sixteen, if my parents were the type of disciplinarians that so many of my schoolmates had. Even today, if people try to hold me back, I walk out. I refuse to be stopped."

When she was fifteen, she met "a darling" Italian boy. They decided to visit his home in Sicily, so they ran away. Ingrid wore her best black leather jacket for the trip. All was well until they reached the Swiss border.

The border guard was all business.

"How old are you, Fraulein?" He was eyeing her passport and she knew there was no use to lie.

"I'm fifteen," she said with what she hoped was a winning smile. He wasn't the type to be won over by a pretty girl.

"Sorry, it is against the law for minors to cross the border," he said sternly.

He advised her to call her parents. The runaway had to remain at the guard station until her parents arrived. Her Italian friend wasn't detained, as he was returning home, but he immediately said he would stay there with her. Ingrid was in a quandary. Call her mother? She would have been beyond furious. She hoped that her father would be more understanding. She called him at his office.

"Hello, Papa? It's Ingrid," she said.

She told him what had happened, and he drove immediately to the border station to rescue her and her friend. She remembers how very happy she was to see him. When he got there, he looked at her with amusement.

"Never wear black leather when you run away, Ingrid," he said with a laugh. "Wear something less conspicuous."

Good advice! And, to his daughter's relief, he didn't tell her mother.

She says that this reaction on her father's part was, once again, like a comrade in arms, which she believes came from their past lives together as World War II soldiers. It was a relationship that she thinks her mother never understood except as being her husband's soft spot for their only daughter.

"But I truly think my relationship to my father was much more than that. And this comradeship continued until his death."

Her father was supportive also, when as a student, Ingrid found unusual solutions for school difficulties.

"For example, if I found myself worrying over undone homework, I would supersede the problem mentally by resolving not to worry until I had reason for it. Mind over matter was a very well known theory, and I used it frequently to positively influence the outcome of tests and to regulate my body weight. Of course, I didn't divulge these methods to either my father or my mother.

"Nor did they know about the little box which I covered with colorful paper. In it I kept secret notes and little personal objects. In a flash of inspiration out of one of my past lives, I once filled a glass with hot water. I threw a fashion finger ring into it and then waited for the ring to melt so I could gild my box. Of course, the ring remained intact. The memory, from one of my past lives, had to do with alchemy in which metals were gilded for use in rituals or to seal secret containers."

Ingrid read all the metaphysical literature she could find, including classical scripts of the world religions such as Hinduism, Buddhism, Islam, Sikh and Jainism. She read about hypnotism, UFO's, psychology, dream analysis, out of body experiences and the lives of mystics and took any opportunity to go to informative lectures about any of these subjects, including those of religious groups, churches and sects.

"I began practicing yoga from a book I read," she says. "I first joined a yoga group and later a meditation group founded by Paramahansa Yogananda. Meditation was part of my daily routine. In the meditations, I often found myself remembering other worlds, other identities, feeling timeless. I would see temples, palaces, cosmic lights, and heavenly bodies. This was the state of consciousness I sought for so long. I felt a deep satisfaction that in this lifetime I had the possibility to intensively pursue my spiritual goals. This indicates that in some previous lifetimes I did not have this possibility or did not appreciate it."

Ingrid explains that since our subconscious is older than our present identities, there are many inexplicable fears, dilemmas and concepts, which have not originated in our present life. Vivid scenes and descriptions such as she has experienced throughout her current lifetime derive largely from the reincarnating components of our subconscious mind.

She points out that everyone has had experiences, used sayings and followed trains of thought which point to their reincarnation.

"As a young student, I became so deeply involved in these mystical studies that I neglected some of the interests pursued by other teens, such as movies, clothes and fun trips. But I would make up for that later.

"I subscribed to Germany's only metaphysical magazine, The Other World. The name was later changed to Esotera. This same magazine many years later has published several articles about my own work in past life therapy."

Languages also played an important role in Ingrid's life. Early on, she discovered a talent in learning foreign languages. She studied French in school, although she had taught herself much of the vocabulary prior to her formal studies.

At thirteen, she voluntarily enrolled in an evening Italian language class. She had to travel into the city by bus two nights a week to attend it.

"I became fascinated by Unidentified Flying Objects when I was fourteen," she says. "I tried to use telepathy to attract UFO's. One night, I woke up from a deep sleep. The church bell was ringing three bells indicating it was 3:00 a.m. Looking out the window of my bedroom, directly across from my bed, I saw an oblong object beside the moon. This thing, whatever it was, was double the size of the moon. Over and over again, I saw it fill up with light from its top to its bottom and then go back to black.

"I tried to get up out of bed to watch it more closely, but I couldn't move. It was as if a force field was holding me down. The sense of being immobile seems to be a common experience when UFOs are present. As the object moved slowly to the right and disappeared, I again heard the peal of the church bell. It was a solitary bong announced 3:15 a.m. I fell back asleep in awe at what I had seen."

The next day, she read the newspaper thoroughly to see what others had written about the night before. She was surprised to find there was nothing about it. At school, she asked fellow students if they had seen the strange object in the sky. Nobody had seen a thing. Many years later, she read somewhere that space ships actually do this. They change from matter to anti- matter, and from black to white as they do so.

"Ah well," she says, "That was my last attempt to contact a space ship. Soon, I found myself again engrossed in Asian culture and people. I was awestruck by Asian people on the TV and fascinated by the martial arts. It all somehow seemed so strangely familiar to me."

"Mama, I've decided to study martial arts," Ingrid said one morning.

If she wondered why her blonde-haired young daughter wanted to take up a rather masculine sport, her mother didn't ask why. She always supported her daughter's endeavors, no matter how wild or fanciful they might seem to others.

"And when do you plan to start this new activity?" she asked.

"Tonight, Mama. I've found a professional martial arts school where they teach a mixture of several styles."

"I'm sure you'll enjoy it, my dear," she said.

And enjoy it, Ingrid did! She plunged in with her usual vigor and quickly passed two belt exams.

Then she heard about another school which was teaching Tae Kwon Do, the Korean form of martial art. Kim Kwang-il, the Korean instructor at this new school, had the reputation of being very tough, but she wasn't afraid. She called and requested to apply at his school.

"You want to learn Tae Kwon Do?" He sounded dubious over the phone. Unlike today, not many girls in the 1960's were taking up martial arts.

"Yes, I've already passed two belts at my present school, and I've heard so much about you," she said.

"Well, I talked him into seeing me. He arranged a private session for me at the school. When I arrived, Master Kim looked me up and down. I'm sure he was wondering why a young girl such as me was so anxious to train with him. He would discover later how adventurous and ambitious I really was."

"Come, let's see what you have learned," he said. "I am ready," she answered with a bow.

"He was surprised at my work during the session that followed. At the end, he told me that I was very good."

"If you come with me, you will have your black belt within two years," he said.

If she would come and study with him? It was another prayer answered! Quickly, she changed schools. She remembers this new school as being much more professional than her last. The training she would get in this Korean school opened up a totally new perspective. She worked out every other night, feeling very masculine in her workouts, and she looked down on the male students because of what she perceived to be their lack of ambition and dedication.

"You're a better student than almost all the male students here," her instructor told her, to her great joy.

"I had the feeling that I had practiced these martial arts before, in a different life." She says.

"And later, when I practiced reincarnation regression, I discovered that indeed I had lived a past life as a highly trained Samurai in Medieval Japan. At sixteen, I knew only that my studies made me very tough and self-confident. And increasingly I longed to visit Asia as I watched all the newly produced martial arts movies."

It was during her hunt for this new martial arts school that she first met her good friend Roland. He was about two years older than she, and he was the secretary for the martial arts school she joined.

Roland taught Yoga at the school in partial payment for his studies there. He wasn't into Karate as Ingrid was, but they became fast friends. She introduced him to her parents who said they thought he was a very fine young man.

She joined his Yoga class. After school, they would sit around and discuss all kinds of metaphysical things. Ingrid was reading the Indian Vedic scriptures: his ambition was to read every metaphysical book in print.

"Of course, there were far fewer such books in those days than there are today. I wanted to learn how to float in space, and he was interested in transcendentalism among other exotic philosophies. We motivated each other in our mutual quest for enlightenment."

Roland indirectly sparked what would become the impetus for their journey to India. "You know, Ingrid, I have read that there are Yoga Masters living in the Himalayas that can appear physically in two places at once," he said in a dreamy voice one afternoon. "I think if we went there we could find such a person," she told him.

They began talking about taking such a trip. In the meantime, they went often to Switzerland to hear lectures about reincarnation, which they both believed in.

Many of these lectures were given in Zurich by the late Elizabeth Haich, an author and lecturer considered a leader in the field. She had founded a Yoga school in Arosa, Switzerland which she managed until her death at the age of 99. When Ingrid knew her, she was a strong, vigorous woman.

"One thing I was especially impressed by in Haich's presentation was her answer during her astrological readings to those asking her what their chart revealed about what they should become in their lives," Ingrid says.

"She would ask 'What would you like to do'? If the person would say 'I would like to be an artist,' she would surprise them. Without even looking at their chart, she would say, 'See, that's exactly what's written in your chart.' Of course, she meant that you don't have to read a chart to follow your heart's desire."

Ingrid and Roland also attended lectures in Winterthur at the temple of the Swami Omkarananda. The temple was painted light blue, a color that is very popular with Asian religions. The Swami would present his lecture and then would meet his audience. Each person could ask him one question. The two of them would return home from these trips feeling very enlightened.

"Because of all these positive experiences, I found myself changing from the shy, silent child I once was," she says. "My livelihood today comes from not only my therapy work but also from the lectures and seminars I give around Europe. It's hard for others to believe I was a youngster who was terrified of talking in front of others in class. As I would learn from my past life studies, the talent was always there, but traumas from earlier lives would stop me from speaking out."

Her route to salvation, she says, was the traveling she would do around the world which gave her the self confidence she needed. She learned that she was okay, no matter where she found herself. Also helping her overcome her insecurities was learning how to tap into the memories and knowledge of her past lives.

"As I have mentioned before," she says, "somehow I am able to pick up languages in a way that the people who speak that language as their mother tongue can hardly notice I was not born in that country.

When I visited Japan at the age of nineteen, for example, I was able to speak Japanese without an accent within four months."

Years later, during her past life studies, she learned that she once was a Chinese diplomat traveling through that country. She remembers in that life losing everything after a night in the bar when she was robbed and stripped of everything. It was part of her job as a political intermediary to be able to speak the different dialects and practice the different customs. In that lifetime, to carry out her diplomatic duties, she traveled all over China in a sedan chair carried by four male servants.

America is another country she loves. She believes this continent is a place where she spent a number of lifetimes.

"Both Canada and the United States have always been good to me," she says, "and my relationship with the American people is excellent and very natural. Often, when I have needed help it was an American who gave it to me.

"I have lived several lifetimes in the United States. During regressions many years later, I remembered being an Irish woman who immigrated to America with her husband in the 17th Century. We arrived after a long and difficult journey, not knowing if we would ever make it safely to port. Many died on the ship, and our physical needs were barely met. After we arrived, we homesteaded land and worked it with our own hands. America turned out to be the Promised Land we had been told about."

Another lifetime was spent in Florida at the turn of the 20th century. In this life, she was the daughter of a rich politician, and had an "illegal" romance with an Indian man.

"We met in the fields at secret places. This man was my ex-husband, Marc, in this, my present lifetime," she says. "My Indian lover was killed in a fight and never returned.

"I felt guilty about this, and I wondered if he had actually been murdered because of our relationship. I discovered that it was a random killing taking place in the turmoil of those times. I remembered that I was very sad about his death and later married a man I didn't love. I then found life constraining and boring and died at the birth of my third child."

Florida has become her second home in her current life. She often spends several months there every year.

She points out that her own experiences in past lives reflect a universal truth.

"When it comes to how we cope with others in this life, I ask you to look into your own lives. Are there not people you have met with whom you had an immediate rapport? And are there not others you instinctively dislike at first sight?" she asks.

"These feelings could be a reaction to your relationships with those people in a past life. If you, yourself, fear speaking out in front of others, it may be because in some past life you were castigated, perhaps even put to death for revealing publically your beliefs.

"Or it might be because you made a terrible mistake, such as rallying troops to a war or battle which was lost and that you accepted the responsibility for its defeat. "

She adds that with help from a past life therapist, you can obtain more insight and knowledge to overcome such fears.

CHAPTER 3

SEARCHING FOR TRUTHS IN ALL THE RIGHT PLACES

"Dieter is coming to visit us," Roland announced one day. "Who is Dieter?" Ingrid asked.

"My teacher," he said almost reverently. "You will love him."

Ingrid says that the "great man" finally got there but she found she wasn't very impressed with him in spite of Roland's outspoken devotion to his hero.

"Dieter was from South America," she remembers. "He was tall and slim, with dark hair and eyes. He was so far into meditation that no everyday conversation was possible with him. He would sit and play the harmonium and meditate. I decided I preferred a teacher whom you can reach on the everyday plane, but Roland thought he had very deep insight.

"Roland was - and is - a dear man. He isn't critical of anybody, and he is so forgiving. I remember how a bus conductor once yelled at him terribly for merely asking for some information. I would have been furious, but Roland simply shook his head and told me 'Maybe I yelled at somebody like that in a past life, and now I'm getting it back'."

Roland and Ingrid used to dream of being locked into one of the Egyptian pyramids to meditate. When years later she actually visited a pyramid, she realized how foolish that dream had been. Dusty and musty smelling, pyramids didn't very seem conducive to a serene, enlightening experience in her opinion.

At the time, though, the two of them were very much into Egyptian lore. They were fascinated by their belief that you should never awaken sleeping people because their astral self would be out of their body and would have to snap back. Such a rude awakening was considered to be unholy. She and Roland even greeted each other, bowing and saying "Namaste" which means in Hindi "I greet the God in you."

They threw themselves into anything spiritual, but they were also addicted to the new wave of martial arts films that were on the market. It was agreed that they must have lived in China in their past lives.

"I know that Roland and I have a Karmic friendship in that we knew each other in past lives. While we are no longer in close contact, I still hear from him occasionally. He continues to teach Yoga and he is becoming quite famous in Europe for teaching memory training techniques," she says to me.

The young couple had big dreams back then, and was determined to make as many of them come true as they could. They discussed all sorts of spiritual issues such as life after death, vegetarianism, reincarnation, magical powers, the Holy Vedic scriptures, Bhagavad Gita and UFO's. She was delighted she could talk about such things with him, and he would answer her adult to adult in spite of their young ages. No idea or concept seemed too far-fetched.

Besides studying with Dieter, Roland was also trained by an Indian Yoga teacher, Swami Dev Murti, who maintained a Yoga school in the Black Forest.

"We should go there to practice meditation and Yoga," urged Roland.

She agreed that it sounded like a wonderful idea, especially since it was quite inexpensive. A small fee covered room, board and meditation studies. And so, her next school vacation found Roland and herself heading off to a chalet in the Black Forest and a two week visit to his Swami.

The chalet, called "Schloss Aubach," lay in the middle of the forest.

"It's so romantic," she breathed, when she first saw it in the woods.

There were no other houses anywhere near them. The chalet stood in a green, grassy area that separated it from the surrounding trees. The air was fragrant from the smells of the forest and the sunshine.

Aubach was called a "schloss" or "castle," but it was actually a very simple castle or chalet, made in the Elizabethan style of dark logs and white cement between.

There were ten guest rooms. Ingrid's was rather small, painted light blue, with windows that let in glorious light. A feather bed stood against one wall and against another was a blue painted Indian chest decorated with brass ornaments to hold her clothes. There was no closet, and the one bathroom was located down a dark, narrow hall. Near the bed was a small table with a wash basin, pitcher and fresh towels.

Downstairs, at the foot of a wooden stairway, was the "gathering room," with old Oriental rugs piled on top of each other. There were no chairs, but Ingrid found that the thick rugs proved to be very comfortable to sit on. The walls were hung with pictures, and there were shelves filled with books. The room had a feeling of light-heartedness and comfort. Their meditations, yoga exercises and lectures were held there.

Roland and Ingrid were part of a group of twelve students attending the program that summer. Days began with a 5:30 a.m. meditation, followed by the serving of a bitter type of tea which was supposed to cleanse their systems. This was followed by a variety of activities, including Yoga exercises and many lectures.

Swami Dev Murti never did appear. It seems he was off traveling abroad somewhere. His wife and son Bal, who was about twenty at the time, ran the school.

Mrs. Swami was somewhere in her forties who always wore beautiful saris. She always supervised the cooking of the meals. The diet was strictly vegetarian and consisted of delicious Indian foods. Even the dogs, who were German Shepherds, were vegetarians and seemed to thrive on this diet, Ingrid noted.

"Bal was very strong. I'll never forget the day he had a truck run over his belly to show how mind works over matter. He wasn't hurt at all. There were a number of newspaper articles written about his feat."

"This is a living example of what Yoga can do for our life style," one of her teachers said.

All the staff were followers of the Swami, including the cooks. The exercise teacher, a woman of about fifty, led them in Hatha Yoga. There was also a young woman who was a massage therapist.

"I never massage strangers," she told Ingrid. "Why not?"

"Because you don't know what bad energy they may have in their bodies," she explained.

She warned Ingrid never to go to a professional massage therapist "because they put sick energy from one person into another."

"Oh, it's true," she said, as Ingrid looked doubtfully at her. "A therapist can certainly transmit energy from one person to another."

"Now, I'm only repeating what she said. I'm sure there are those who might disagree with this theory, but it did make sense to me,' says Ingrid.

"She also told me that "it is the energy and attitude that make people well, not the massage itself."

What impresses her, even after all these years, is the memory of how very centered all these people were.

"I always think of that and even now discuss it in my seminars. I ask them if they live their beliefs or only pretend that they do. "

Ingrid found that with these followers of the Swami, there was no ego. No one spoke much, except what needed to be said, and there was never a bad word spoken. She found a true peace in that chalet. It was her first experience with such a life, and she enthusiastically joined in all of it.

She discovered during the meditations that she got in touch very easily with her immaterial self, but it was hard to come back from this spiritual world into her body afterwards.

"Today, I believe that past life therapy is the best of both worlds. You see, I have found a discrepancy in concentrating only on meditation. During it, you link up with the immaterial world and there is a burden in returning to the physical. You often ask yourself why you must return. In essence, it creates a gap between the spiritual and the physical worlds, with the spiritual seeming so much better. I'm afraid the physical and the spiritual are different in that they don't mesh. It takes some adjustment to get back to everyday life.

"It seems that each of us lives in both the spiritual and physical worlds simultaneously.

Those who say "I only believe in what I see" can be easily challenged. After all, what is objective reality? Even that solid-seeming table is made up of trillions of moving molecules. And what is snow? The Eskimos have at least twenty five words to define it," she points out.

At Schloss Aubach, for the first time in her life, Ingrid found she was able to communicate with people who had truly accomplished something. They had put their beliefs into their every day lives.

"When I was much younger, I had dreams of ending up in a monastery. My experience at Aubach showed me that you can put simple truths into your life without traveling to the Himalayas or living in a cave."

The Swami's disciples taught her about Prana energy. Everyone has it. It's "life energy." The students were taught deep breathing exercises to release oxygen - and this energy - to flow through our body.

Physical exercise was taught which opens the spine and relaxes the muscles and allows this "life energy" to flow through the human body.

At the chalet Ingrid and Roland were taught the seven chakras of the body, which is the energy that, once freed, moves from the base of your spine to your head, releasing enlightenment and tremendous energy throughout your body.

These chakras are the centers of life force. The first is the Kundalini chakra, which is known as the base and is located in the lower spine. The second is the sacral plexus which is situated in the lower abdomen behind and approximately two inches from the belly button. The third is the solar plexus found at the base of the rib cage; the fourth, called the heart plexus lies near the heart while the fifth is the throat plexus found at the base of the neck in the throat. The sixth is in the middle of the brow and is known as the third eye and the seventh is located at the top of the head and is the crown plexus. When you learn to tap into them, you succeed in tapping into your life energy.

The Swami's cooks, two British monk-like men, proved to be experts in these breathing exercises. They would lead the students outside every morning onto the green lawn.

"People always say what nice air, but they never breathe it in," their exercise teacher would say.

"Let's take in as much as we can of what God has given us in abundance," he would add. During one of the lectures, a woman in the group asked if humans reincarnate as animals. "Well, if he thought and lived like a dog, he can," he said.

"I personally think an animal can be better than a person, so I don't think reincarnation as a dog is a step back. It would be an important experience that could be lived through that dog's body," observes Ingrid.

They were taught that one's body is a vessel which needed to be kept clean, and free of poisons, such as meat. Meat, the teachers explained, is harmful because of the suffering of the animal slaughtered. Because animals are killed under stress, they said, we take its trauma as well as its fear which releases unhealthy hormones into our own bodies.

It was at this point in Ingrid's life that she decided to become a vegetarian.

"After I did so, I became increasingly calmer. I have tried to eat meat on occasion only to discover every time I either become very shaky or very lethargic. And today's meat we buy in the market is admittedly full of added hormones and antibiotics, none of which is very good for us."

She says that she became and stayed a vegetarian because she grew convinced this was a more healthy and ethical way to feed oneself.

"I suppose another thing that sold me on a vegetarian life was how radiant the Swami's people all were with their clear, smooth skin and how young they all looked, even those over 50. But the ultimate proof is my own experience and the well being of my body. There is this myth that vegetarians have no force or strength. I have practiced martial arts for years, and I continue to do so now that I am nearing 60. No strength? No force? Definitely not true, and I am living proof of that!

Some of the things she and Roland were taught during those two weeks were: you are what you eat; watch your thoughts for they are what you are; don't be too extreme but rather try to live a balanced life; have a healthy family life; don't become a fanatic about anything but stay in the middle; try not to be angry with poisonous thought and words because all that will come back to you; and, most importantly, remember that what you send out to others you will receive back.

All too soon, their two week stay with the Swami's people was over, and Roland and Ingrid returned to Stuttgart to resume their "normal" lives. Her parents were a little taken aback about her vegetarian diet, but they soon adjusted. Her mother said it was cheaper, anyway, considering what meat cost in the marketplace.

Ingrid graduated from high school at fifteen, two years ahead of her class. In Germany, there are four years of primary grades, six years of middle school, and three more years at high school. Students then take an examination in order to go to the University. Ingrid enrolled in a business school, but after three months found that she couldn't stand it.

"I'm like a flower without water," she complained to her father. "I hate that school. It's not the right place for me."

She wanted, instead, to study languages privately. Her father agreed to this because he knew if she didn't like something, she wouldn't do it well. So he sent her to the Berlitz School where she studied French, English and Italian for a year. She passed all the exams and graduated.

During that time, she also took business courses on the side. By this time, she was ready to go to work as a secretary for firms dealing with foreign countries.

"At one point, Roland and I both studied the Hindi language. Knowing this, some friends asked me to translate the lectures of an Indian Sikh master from English into German during the man's visit to Germany. Among the reasons they gave for this request was my knowledge of the Hindi culture, my experience with Yoga and my fluency in the English language."

The Sikh master turned out to be a dignified, wise old gentleman who gave very interesting and profound speeches in English. To Ingrid's delight, the two of them indulged in intellectual discourses about the states of consciousness that could be achieved through the spiritual path. She learned that the Sikh religion contains many analytical elements, and knowledge of the spiritual plane invokes life for us on Earth to be more Godly and devoted.

A strong authority figure, this Sikh master liked to gather around him those people who were ready to receive his messages and follow him. He had the idea that Ingrid, too, should become one of these followers, but she says that something held her back.

"Deep in my heart, I was not convinced that this person was my master and he seemed to realize how I felt."

"Very well, my young memsahib," he said the last day they met. He looked disappointment at her obvious lack of interest. "But perhaps one day you will visit me in India?"

"Of course," she promised him.

It was a promise that she would keep at seventeen.

CHAPTER 4

ANSWERS MAY LIE IN MYSTICAL INDIA

"Mama, do you think Papa would let me go to India?" Ingrid asked one day.

"You want to go where? When?" Her mother looked at Ingrid in amazement.

"I've been studying Hindi for ages now, Mama, and I know I'd get by just fine."

"Darling, you aren't even seventeen yet. Who would go with you."

"Mama! I'll be seventeen in just a couple of months. And I'm a big girl. I can go alone," Despite her young age, she was as usual very sure of herself.

"Not alone, Ingrid," her mother said firmly.

Ingrid remembers, "Well, it took some talking, first with Mama and then with Papa, but they finally gave in to me and agreed to the trip, especially since Roland, spurred by my initiative, decided to come, too. My parents liked him very much, and they felt I would be safe with him along.

"My parents had no reason not to trust me. I wasn't the type to get drunk, and I was mature for my age. I had always been a very good student, I was very driven and I knew exactly what I wanted. It was also obvious to them that I was pursuing something very important to me."

Her father wrote a notarized letter for her to carry stating that she was authorized to travel on her own and that she was not a runaway.

"Actually, I never used that letter once. I also carried with me two addresses. One was of the family of my Hindi teacher in Bombay who was informed of my arrival and the other was of that Sikh Yoga professor in Chandigarh for whom I had translated several lectures when he visited Germany earlier."

Ingrid was delirious with anticipation when her plane lifted up over her homeland and headed toward magical India. It was her first independent trip not connected with family, and that made it a huge step to adulthood, in her opinion.

"That trip to India was one of the peak excitements of my life. Finally, I would explore the country where so much wisdom and ancient knowledge had originated. I had the highest expectations to meet masters and saints and to encounter spirituality firsthand. Since this was such an important journey, Roland and I agreed to follow our own pursuits and to explore according to our inner calling.

"We were determined to find the right Master and the Ashram that would lead us to enlightenment. We had different ideas about finding this Ashram, as it turned out."

"Now, remember, when we get to Bombay, I have several places I want to see and I know you have other places you want to go," she told Roland.

Bombay, now called Mumbai, was a large, bustling city and the two young people were excited to arrive there. They went sightseeing. Her Hindi teacher's family visited them. And of course they meditated every day.

"But after three days, I was fed up with that. I wanted to travel around the country. Roland, on the other hand, was satisfied with just staying there and meditating," Ingrid says.

"Well, I'm not staying here," she told him. "There are too many places I want to see." "Oh, I don't think that would be a good idea, Ingrid. I promised your parents to look out for you," he protested.

But Ingrid was persistent, as she always is when she sets her mind on doing something despite any possible disapproval.

After some discussion, he reluctantly agreed it might be better if they separated. "I'll see you in six weeks," she said.

"That was when we were to return home to Germany. But at that moment I was ready to finally taste my first great freedom! I would go to Delhi alone.

"Have you ever traveled by train in India? What an experience! It is very dusty, very crowded and very hard to buy a ticket to ensure a seat due to endless chaotic line-ups at the ticket counters."

After finally getting to the head of a line, she was able to obtain a ticket, board the train and find her seat.

"I sat down and breathed deeply. It did not smell like cool, clean Germany. The odor of animals that were also brought on board with us as well as the smell of curry exhaled by my fellow passengers permeated the air. The travelers were dressed in all manners of clothing from the typical saris of the women to the occasional Western wear of tourists such as me. I promised myself that I would get and wear a sari and a kurta (a colorful, embroidered shirt and pants set) as soon as possible."

"You are traveling alone, yes, memsahib?"

Ingrid opened her eyes to see a young woman smiling at her. She was sitting across from her and dressed in a beautifully embroidered golden sari.

"Yes," Ingrid said.

"She seemed excited to learn that I was from Germany. She had never been there, and she was enthralled to meet someone from so far away. We struck up a conversation. She, too, was going to Delhi where she lived. By the time we reached that city, I was invited to her home for dinner. And she wasn't the only one who would invite me to visit. The hospitality of the people of India is striking. I found the Indian women very self confident, feminine and without the vanity of Western women."

In Delhi, Ingrid went native. She immediately bought and began to wear the saris and other native clothing. Along with her other purchases, she bought a sitar, a famous Indian musical instrument, and took lessons to learn how to play that country's music. She also learned their dances.

"I identified fully with the Indian way of life," she says.

By now a strong believer in reincarnation, she was thrilled to discover another of her past lives.

"I remembered I had lived it in Sarnath, the Buddha's birthplace. In that lifetime, I was a wandering monk who followed the teachings of The Buddha and strove for enlightenment. It was one that was filled with meditation, prayer, and wandering from temple to temple. I lived one day at a time then. Every moment was precious and intensely experienced. I must say that was one of my most spiritually developed lifetimes."

Ingrid explains that "Buddhism is a profound philosophy. Through it, we learn that where there is enlightenment and conscious clarification, obstacles which stand in the way of our inward liberation simply disappear. It is a religious philosophy which has important symbolisms of opposites: ignorance and wisdom.

"Ignorance means not knowing the true causes which underlie the restrictions and limitations under which we live and suffer. Wisdom, then, means you comprehend all the tragic moments the soul encounters. The more this ignorance changes into self realization, the more we can understand and be aware of our present circumstances.

"Everybody has probably at least heard of "karma." Karma is our personal experience of the fruits of our own thinking, intentions and actions. It is the harvesting of consequences in our past actions and of the attitudes which led up to those actions. We are the sum total and the result of all our former deeds and decisions."

In India, she learned that "Buddhism teaches us that the consequences of our own actions come under a law which must be obeyed. It is the world's own law of causality. It is only in the light of this timelessness that we can grasp the Buddhist theory that man must also bear responsibility for those fateful events which are incomprehensible to us and which we do not believe we could ever have caused.

"Accordingly, the events and troubles of this life come not only from current or earlier actions in this life, but also from the causes of action by us in earlier lives. And our future Karma depends on what we do in our present life."

At seventeen, Ingrid found herself absorbing Indian culture and beliefs into every pore of her body during those few, precious weeks she spent there.

"There were so many temples in that country! Some were simple and others luxurious, but they were always colorful and full of spiritual energy. You could meditate there or meet a singing crowd or watch the saints performing their rituals. Sometimes these seers, hermits and gurus would give me a wise piece of advice, or they would read my past and future."

She felt showered by the friendliness of the people she met.

"The only disappointment came from my visit to the Sikh professor. He hadn't changed, but my perception had deepened. I saw in him a man looking for disciples to follow him blindly. He was a man with a tremendous ego, a human weakness which a true Master would not have.

"I asked myself if I should be more humble and accepting or was it the 'Master' who had the difficulty. He demanded that I surrender myself fully to his guidance and his power to make all decisions for me. If I had done so, I would have soon become a totally passive, obedient person."

This was not an idea that Ingrid found appealing. Something deep inside told her that no, she was not going to play the disciple to someone who was not really above others but was human, too.

"It was as if my umbilical cord was again being cut, and I felt a deep sense of disillusionment. I left him after that week-long visit and never saw him again."

In the beautiful vale of Kashmir, she finally found her true spiritual leader, Swami Shivananda Saraswati who, she says, helped link her up with her inner path. Ingrid met him through a mutual friend, Govinda during her visit to Delhi. At the time she met him, she didn't know he was a Master.

Invited to a party at Govinda's, she was met at the door by her host who seemed more excited than usual.

"We are very honored today, memsahib. The Swami Shivananda Saraswati is among our guests. Come. I will introduce you," he said, leading her to an imposing man.

About five feet five in height, the Swami was heavy set and wore the white Shiva lines and two red dots on his forehead. A white gown was wrapped around his body. Ingrid was immediately struck by the man's commanding presence. She would soon learn that his mind centered upon the spiritual level and he had no ego, unlike that shown by her Sikh professor.

"We had a long conversation that day. Since he spoke no English, we communicated in Hindi and occasionally through an interpreter. I told him about my Yogi exercises and my interest in the spiritual way of life."

He looked deeply into her eyes.

"Come to my temple and you will learn of these things, young memsahib," he said.

"He had deep-set brown eyes that were both warm and kind, and I knew I had to find out what he could teach me. A few days later, I went by bus to his Temple in Kashmir where he met me. In the days that followed, I saw him always in meditation, linked to another world, even when he was talking to others. We meditated together."

One of these lay in concentrating on moving along their spine with certain images. He would thump gently on her forehead to open her third eye, and he taught her that when you are "centered," you can open your chakras fully to accept all kinds of energy and strength.

He told her to spend several weeks at a time concentrating on one chakra, and he taught her how to focus.

"My daughter, first you must sit down and relax. Do your deep breathing exercise in and out, very slowly. Try to breathe in one nostril and then the other. When you are breathing in balance, you will have steady, deep, relaxed breaths. As you do this, turn your attention inward to the area you wish to concentrate on."

She would do as she was told.

"Now, try to be still and go deeper and deeper into that awareness."

When she did, she would have variable types of mental experiences. Sometimes she would visualize images, scenarios of places she had never been in this her present life. At other times, she would see vivid colors and experience strange feelings. During those exercises, her mind was in a different state.

"It was fruitful to try to stay in that exercise for about thirty minutes at a time. Usually, I started with a physical exercise such as Hatha Yoga and then did my meditation. In this case, my meditation was focused on opening my chakra. It was like another layer of being opening for me, and it created for me a timeless state of beingness. It was also strength-oriented."

She explains that when you do this exercise, you will find that your body feels very invigorated at the end. It offers much more energy, compared to other types of meditations, allowing you to float in space and tap more and more into yourself.

The Swami was a follower of Shiva, the deity of destruction. The trinity of creation, preservation and destruction is represented through the Gods Brahma, Vishnu and Shiva. In this philosophy, there is no new life until something ends or is dissolved.

Wearing only one sheet of cloth and sandals, the Swami led expeditions to the holy sites of Shiva in the grottos and caves of the snowy Himalayas. Ingrid reports that although he spoke very little, he was an extremely strong man who had mastered his body completely. He did not feel the cold nor did he depend on food and drink to sustain him. He communicated through his body and through meditation.

While he gave her advice on cleansing techniques for the body, health, diet and meditation, he didn't burden her with moral advice.

"As young as I was, I could easily detect vanity and egotistic notions within the so-called wise men and Masters and would not fall for them. This Master, however, was a great example of finding the absolute peace within, to be totally independent of all biological functions and, above all, of worldly opinion. He was what I call self-centered or resting in himself. He was balanced and did what he was lead to do, traveling extensively throughout much of India."

"He had unlimited physical resources, had no ties to anyone and seldom engaged in any social activities other than those related to meditation and worship. He was always open to the questions and needs of people who wanted to follow the spiritual path, but he did not establish any links other than the guidance to higher awareness levels.

"During this time with him, I decided what the priorities of my life would be. I determined that I would follow my destiny, no matter where it led me. One secret of life that I learned then, to be reinforced often throughout my life, is the secret of personal success. It is very simple. The key to long-term success in your life is to do what you want to do. Your talents and interests are your guidelines and will steer you toward fulfillment. Everything else, including money and opportunity, will fall into place."

Later in her life, during her own seminars, when young people asked Ingrid what profession they should choose, she followed the lead of the great Elizabeth Haich and asked them "Well, what do you like to do most?" And if they said "I would like to be a musician," Her answer was "whatever interests you is a calling and has an inner task. Our future is up to us. We must have enough faith to follow our stars."

Ingrid Valliere's philosophy is "If we say we haven't the money or the time to do what we really want to do, we are only making excuses. We don't really want it badly enough. We do what we want to do, IF we want it badly enough. We can always find the way, whether it's a promotion at work, the chance to go to university or take that trip abroad. If we can't come up with the means to do it, then either we don't need it or life has something else in store for us."

She believes strongly in what she calls the LAW OF PROSPERITY. These laws of prosperity state that in order to get what you want you first have to be very clear of what it is that you REALLY want and then give it life - can you imagine to experience it with all your senses? Can you visualize yourself already there?

Mind over matter - all manifestation in form of money, dreams fulfilled, possessions in the physical universe have first been created in the mind, so again before putting yourself at work to implement these ideas they should have a strong mental force behind them. You need self-confidence and self-worth to reap your riches and need to trust the universe it will bring whatever suits your well-being and progress as a human being. WE GET WHAT WE BELIEVE WE DESERVE!

She believes that we are all born to learn certain tasks in this lifetime, and we bring certain tools with us, but how we complete our tasks or even if we do so is up to us.

She and her Swami talked about evil. Among these conversations was a discussion of how people become serial murderers.

"We agreed that this murderer may have been a victim himself in a previous life if not in his present one. Crime is a route leading to something else, whether an attempt to rid oneself of something, gaining a material good or seeking peace of mind. Evil people are just looking for something such as ego satisfaction, self preservation or power but doing it in the wrong way. All human intentions are good although the methods of some are not. I learned much about life and human destiny from the Swami."

Too soon, her six-week visit to India came to an end. How quickly it had passed! She returned to Bombay and Roland. He was enthralled by her tales of her adventures.

"Well, perhaps I should have gone with you," he said regretfully, as they flew back to Stuttgart.

On the plane trip home, Ingrid chose to wear one of her beautiful Indian saris. She also made up her face to look Indian.

Her mother met her at the airport.

"Ingrid? Is that you?" She looked her daughter over with some amusement. "I thought you were some visitor from India."

"Did I really fool you, Mama?"

"Absolutely." Her mother smiled as she fingered the embroidery on Ingrid's sari. "What a beautiful costume."

Now back home in Stuttgart and finished with her formal schooling, Ingrid sought paying work and the furthering of her private interests.

"I took a job as a foreign language secretary in the export department of a large company. In my spare time, I continued my training in the martial arts. I also took up Indian dance from a native woman instructor who had studied under the world famous dancer Uday Shankar. I enjoyed my dancing very much because it contained many religious ideas and different dynamics of temperamental expression."

Besides practicing Tae Kwon Do three times a week and dancing one to two times a week, she also walked for miles. She enjoyed walking very fast.

Sometimes she walked with friends who would puff "Wait up, you slave master," as they tried to keep up with her long strides. "My feet are hurting me and you're walking so fast I can't even keep up." They would protest to no avail.

"Needless to say, I often took solitary walks. Then I could go as fast as I wanted with no complaints! In my last lifetime, which was as a World War II soldier, I had to depend on my feet to take me long distances. Otherwise, I could not survive. In that military lifetime, I marched from Czechoslovakia to Cologne, about a thousand kilometers, as part of the war maneuvers.

And during my lifetime as a Samurai, I was on my feet all my life as I walked throughout the country as a spy for the Emperor."

She read extensively. One day, she picked up the autobiography of Paramahansa Yogananda.

"It was a wonderful book, a classic which makes all the supernatural phenomena seem real and the spiritual path attainable. And that is how I came to join the Self Realization Fellowship."

She learned that there was a chapter in Stuttgart and called the name listed. A very gentle couple who led the local group invited her to their home. There she joined fellow practitioners on a weekly basis to meditate together and to listen to Yogananda's speeches or his music.

She learned from Yogananda's writings about the "Om" sound which you are supposed to hear during meditation after you reach a certain level.

"Can you hear the Om after six months?" she asked the group leaders.

She was told that hearing the "Om" wasn't as important as getting on with one's path and meditating regularly.

"During my own therapeutic work, I am often asked that same question – can I solve this difficulty in one month? I tell my clients that a problem is an indication that something needs to be changed in your life. How much time it takes is not as important as that you resolve it in the best way possible for you."

There is no shortcut available, according to Ingrid.

"Trying to put a quick ending to your distress doesn't allow the process to evolve. Difficulties are really never over, but we can use them by tuning into their potential. For example, say you have a fear of expressing yourself. This fear isn't overcome when you finally can speak out in public.

"You can take away your fear, if you accept the challenge to use it for the good. The vexation then is handled and its potential is used." Ingrid likens the transformation from difficulty to potential as a spiral. The problem whirls around and becomes the solution.

CHAPTER 5

THOSE FARAWAY PLACES

Ingrid's trip to India had whetted her appetite for more travel. She began saving her money and making plans for her next trip. She would go from India to Thailand, then Hong Kong, Japan and finally Korea.

During this time she worked as a foreign language secretary in an export department of a big company. Secretaries, especially good ones, were hard to find in Germany in 1972, therefore they were given many special perks, such as taking extended vacations. Ingrid said her superiors considered her to be a very good secretary.

"One day at lunch, I saw a young, very pretty, olive-skinned woman. She was new to the company, so I sat down and had lunch with her. Her name was Surya and she had just arrived from Bangkok, Thailand. Like me, she was very ambitious and couldn't wait to travel and see the world. Her life's dream had been to come to Europe, while mine was to visit her country among others in the Far East."

The two young women became immediate friends. Ingrid helped Surya learn about German life, and Surya, in turn, told tales about her own country. An excited Ingrid could hardly wait to see these wonders for herself.

"After my second year of employment, I was ready. I filed with my company for an unpaid leave of four months. Back then, secretaries were in such high demand that companies would agree to almost anything to keep a good one. I had no difficulty in receiving permission to take three months longer than the usual one month leave."

She was now nineteen, and this time there was no doubt that she was old enough to travel alone.

She found India as interesting on this second trip as she had the first time. She planned to travel not only to places she had visited on her previous trip but to new ones as well. Her itinerary included Benares and Calcutta.

"Along the way, I would make new friends and was even more reconfirmed in my desires to continue my spiritual path," she says.

"I visited my spiritual leader, Swami Shivananda Saraswati, in Kashmir before heading for Bangkok where I intended to spend only four days visiting with Surya's family and exploring her exotic city. But then I met Phayong."

"It was midnight when Ingrid arrived at Bangkok Airport. She found it to be very old, primitive and unorganized. The air was thick with the smell of perfumed incense burners which she soon learned were lit to kill mosquitoes. While the long trip had left her a little tired, it didn't matter. She was more invigorated with the excitement about what she would experience next.

"I was directed to the immigration office. I walked in and found Phayong, this totally gorgeous young man who was standing behind the counter."

Tall and slim, he looked like the officer he was. She was immediately attracted by his good looks, but all she said was "Hello."

"Have you anything to declare?" he asked. "No" she said softly,"

He seemed startled and then he really looked at her. Ingrid smiled at him, and he returned her smile."

"You are traveling alone? A beautiful young lady like you? Where is your husband or your father?" he asked.

She told him that there was no husband, and her father was in Germany. "In which hotel are you staying?

"I don't have a reservation anywhere."

He smiled at her. "I'll be off in twenty minutes and I would be glad to take you to the city," he said. "A beautiful young girl as you shouldn't be alone in a strange city at this hour. Let me drive you to a hotel and make sure you are safe."

"It has always been my experience that Asian men are trustworthy, so of course I said yes, immediately," says Ingrid.

During that trip into the city, he asked her about herself and why she chose to travel alone. He was twenty nine, unmarried and with a promising future in Thailand's immigration service.

"It was a good thing he was with me when we reached the hotel. Although it was fairly modern, its staff didn't speak English or German and I knew hardly any words in their language yet."

Phayong saw her to her room and promised to come back the next day to show her around the city.

"Over the next few days, he lived up to his word. He showed me the real Bangkok that tourists seldom see as well as its more familiar attractions. The city at that time was generously built, clean and spacious, not like it is today. Now it is tremendously crowded, with polluted air from the vehicles that fill its streets."

She also spent some time with her friend Surya's family. She found their home to be very beautiful, with pathways, a wooden bridge and a beautiful garden. It was very much like some of the lovely homes she later would visit in Florida.

"While I was with them, Surya's sister gave me an exquisite ring, with a big, dark blue sapphire mounted in gold tapestry. I didn't realize its true value until much later, but she gave it to me because of my friendship to her sister. Asian people are so appreciative!"

In the meantime, Phayong and Ingrid became lovers.

"He was passionate and adoring and I was swept up in the romance of an exotic love amidst the beauty of Thailand. It was a very easy relationship and an exotic experience, living in that new, exciting, beautiful world with him. I'm afraid, however, that my Thai lover loved me much more than I did him. It was, after all, 1972, the middle of the sexual revolution in Europe and the United States. Phayong, however, was from a different world."

She stretched her stay in Bangkok from one to two and a half weeks, until the German embassy told her she could no longer extend her visa.

"Ingrid, darling, you don't have to leave," Phayong implored her on their last night together.

"But I had to continue my journey, despite his pleas. I had a whole world waiting for me to discover, and it didn't include a husband and children."

They met again years later in Stuttgart when he went to Germany as part of a group of Thai immigration officials. He remembered her name and her city and went to the police department looking for her name.

"They put him in touch with my parents, and Mama called me. We had a wonderful visit reminiscing about old times."

CHAPTER 6

HER GEISHA PAST IS CALLING

Before flying to Japan, Ingrid detoured to Hong Kong thinking it might be fun to land a part in a martial arts film. Once there, she discovered that actors need agents and contacts to get cast in movies and she hadn't any. She soon found herself disenchanted with the area. The hustle and bustle of the island city was a tremendous contrast to Thailand's calm pace.

"Four days of Hong Kong was quite enough for me. It was far too commercial for my tastes. Happily, I boarded the plane to Tokyo."

As the plane circled for a landing at Tokyo's airport, Ingrid says she was so excited she could hardly bear the wait. She had yearned for this day for so long. Although she had already learned some basic Japanese from a Korean friend in Germany who spoke the language fluently, when she overheard the Japanese passengers on the plane talking together, she found that she couldn't understand a single word.

Ingrid has always had the ability to make friends with people in uniform and suspects this is because of her many incarnations as officials of various eras. During this flight, she became very good friends with the Egyptian flight crew. She was flying with Egypt Air which then was the most inexpensive air travel.

"Where will you be staying in Tokyo?" one of the stewards asked her.

"Well," she said, "I have addresses of two families who are friends of friends of mine, but I don't have a hotel reservation anywhere."

"Perhaps you could stay at our hotel," he suggested. "You can ride with us on our crew bus."

She accepted the offer gratefully. It would save her the trouble of finding hey way to the hotel on her own.

"When we got on the bus, I was amused to see that the driver was wearing spotless white gloves. I subsequently learned that all bus and taxi drivers in Tokyo wear such gloves, "she says.

She was a little disappointed on her ride to the hotel, as the route didn't take them past any typical Japanese houses or gardens. On the contrary, all the concrete buildings looked quite grey and dull. Somehow, she had expected a more Oriental setting.

The hotel was large and modern, and a room was available. Ingrid checked in and called Hiroshi, the first of the two Japanese people on her list. He was a friend of a Japanese couple she had met at a fair in Stuttgart. They had invited her to their home several times for Japanese dinners.

"I will come to you tomorrow and maybe we can find accommodations more suitable for your budget," Hiroshi promised during their brief conversation during which she had explained to him her limited budget. By then, her trip money was dwindling, and she had only $1,500 left for her whole trip.

True to his word, the next day he came over and moved her into a youth hostel. Youth hostels then charged about one U.S. dollar a night and were very affordable. Enjoying a more typical Japanese lifestyle with her move, she set out to explore Tokyo and her surroundings.

"Those Japanese language lessons I'd taken in Germany didn't help me a bit," she says.

"I couldn't understand anything said in Japanese, although I soon learned some useful phrases. What helped were the students who would walk up to me on a street or in a park and ask me if they could speak English with me. In their schools, they only learned how to read and write English, and now they wanted to practice - on me. So I practiced my limited Japanese on them in return."

Ingrid soon learned to get around Tokyo on its subways and trains. The Japanese people were very helpful when she couldn't find the right destination on the ticket machine. That was because the station names were usually all in Japanese characters, and totally impossible for a foreigner to decipher.

She wandered through museums and parks, finding beautiful Buddhist and Shinto temples inside the magnificently landscaped parks. Often, stone lanterns led the way to the temples.

"No matter what Asian country I visited, the temples always fascinated me. I could spend hours in them, meditating or just contemplating. It all seemed so familiar to me, as though I had spent other lifetimes in such surroundings. I discovered that my current identity of Ingrid would vanish during those hours and a different personality would emerge. This new one was very serious, dedicated with a timeless quality.

"I could feel the lifetimes I'd spent in such temples, and now I was in contact with them again. It was rather like visiting your old school as an adult and finding the memories flooding back to you. The museums also awakened memories with their paintings, temple relics, stone pieces and other art objects. Often, I would spend a full day in one of these museums, soaking in the impressions, feelings and images emanating from these art pieces."

Some part of her felt totally at home in Japan. The Asian values of discipline, respect for life, strength and dignity, tenacity and performance orientation seemed much like her own set of values.

"I felt my very blood exchanging with new blood. A dazzling, exciting new world opened its doors to me. Japanese culture entered my blood like a drug. I felt a longing to stay on that soil and in that world which made me feel self-confident.

"And it was such a familiar world to me! One day, as I walked through an unfamiliar section of Tokyo with a guide, I became dizzy with an intense sense of déjà vu."

"I can tell you what we'll find around that corner," I told my guide. "I described to him what I felt was there. When we turned the corner, it was just as I had predicted. Were the barriers between my present and previous existences breaking down? Had I really walked these streets in previous lifetimes?"

She called and left a message for Yoshifumi, the second Japanese person on her list. He contacted her at the hostel and invited her to stay in his home with him and his wife who was pregnant at the time. Although the woman spoke only Japanese, her husband spoke some German, as he had once lived in Germany for a while. Hiroshi, her other Japanese friend, also spoke German, so they were both helpful in directing her to places she might never have found on her own.

Yoshifumi accompanied her to Kamakura, the place of the giant Buddha and to Nikko, which has one of the fanciest palace-like temples in Japan.

Ingrid soon learned that if you wanted to walk around and enjoy the sight or the artifacts of the temples that the best time to do this was between 6:00 a.m. and 7:00 a.m. After that time, the places would be swarming with thousands of Japanese tourists and school children. School buses would line up by the dozens in the parking lots of such places.

"Japan is one of the originators of the martial arts. Now that I was actually living there, I yearned to visit one of these original schools. The Conservative University of the Martial Arts in Tokyo was considered to be excellent but impossible for visitors or foreigners to enter."

"Don't worry," Yoshifumi told her.

One afternoon, he prepared a roll of rice paper and, in Japanese brush paint, wrote a very polite and official letter to the Headmaster of the University. In it, he explained that Ingrid had come all the way to Japan to study the martial arts and to please grant her access to their educational center. Then he sealed and beautifully wrapped the paper roll with a ribbon bow.

Thus armed, she took the train and arrived at the Conservative University. At the entrance, she handed the paper over to the black uniformed entrance guard. He took the message and disappeared.

"How strangely familiar it all seemed to me. You've been here before. The thought flashed through my mind in an instant. But when? I had never seen this place before - in this lifetime, anyway."

Some years later, during a regression session, she learned why it had all seemed so familiar.

"In that long ago lifetime, I was the male leader of a Japanese martial troop, a group of extremely well disciplined and hardened men, called Samurai, who placed their lives at the service of the emperor. We went around the country seeking out spies and enemies of the emperor and destroyed them. There was no place for sentiment or frivolity, which would have meant death. I also learned that I spent another lifetime as a female Ninja."

Now in modern day Japan, she waited patiently to be admitted by the black uniformed guard to the university. He reappeared fifteen minutes later with another man.

"Welcome," the second man said in English.

He led her into a large hall where the annual National Kendo Championships were underway. Five University officials sat in front of the audience. Ingrid was ushered to sit beside them. In front of them, a hundred or more black-clad Kendo students sat on the floor and watched the ongoing tournament fights.

"I am honored," she told the English-speaking official. "I never expected the honor of attending such an important event."

He then presented her with a Kendo uniform, the headgear, gloves and wooden sword.

The students on the floor giggled about that, but they welcomed the diversion from the hours and hours of combat they had been witnessing.

After the tournament ended, pictures of Ingrid and the winner, Miss Takahashi were taken and later printed in the University's magazine. Later, she was shown through the entire school and watched Judo and Karate lessons and felt part of the ancient martial arts world as practiced by modern young people just like her.

Finally, toward evening, she left the university. It was an enormously meaningful day for the young German girl.

"How was your visit?" Yoshifumi asked when she returned to their home that night. "It was incredible," she said, and regaled him about everything that had happened that magical day.

Shortly after that, Ingrid left Tokyo and traveled by train south through Kyoto, Nara, Osaka, Hiroshima and the island of Kyushu. Since she was allowed to leave some of her luggage at Yoshifumi's home, she was able to travel light.

She stayed at youth hostels, where the Japanese and foreign visitors exchanged songs and stories. After breakfast, she would leave the hostel and travel to the next city or town. Kyoto and Nara were especially interesting. There, she wandered the streets where the geishas were educated and where they would perform in public.

Again, she suffered déjà vu, the certainty she had been there before. The wooden houses and the small, quiet streets seemed as familiar as the peculiar clapping sound on the ground of the high-heel "geta" shoes worn by the Japanese women. The women walked with a swaying motion caused by tight kimonos which didn't leave much room for taking walking steps.

In regression, she would later learn that there was a good reason for this feeling of déjà vu: she had spent a lifetime as a Geisha several centuries ago.

"That lifetime took place in the 15th century. I was a highly trained Geisha in Kyoto and one of the most desired ones, due to my skill in the arts of singing and playing various instruments and my dancing.

"My father in that life was a high official who served the Emperor. It was a privilege to be entertained by me, for my services promised good luck and success to the men who came in contact with me. It was almost a political issue.

"I was considered to be in high standing and, although a woman, had quite some power over these men. They tried to earn my favors and my respect, hoping to succeed politically by making the right connections. I played a key role as both communicator and intermediary."

While in Kyoto, staying in the typical Japanese places with rice paper sliding doors, surrounded by beautiful gardens, Ingrid found herself writing Haiku, the classical Japanese poems. They seemed to flow out of her pen and were about such things as nature, the blossoms and the sun. It seemed to go with a former Geisha life, because all their life was spent indoors, learning music and poetry.

During her travels, she teamed up with other young people to visit temples, castles and parks.

"I loved visiting the Zen temples, which were kept impeccable. There was a timeless spirit within them. The monks who took care of the temples appeared transparent and bodiless. The temple gardens invited one to simply sit and meditate. They were, in fact, a meditation in themselves."

In Kyoto, she was invited to stay in such a temple for a few days. This was quite unusual, since there were only certain temples that would allow outside visitors to stay during certain times of the year. Her quarters were very clean, yet Spartan-like. Food was very scarce and it was taken as part of a daily ritual. Every morsel of rice was eaten, and nothing was wasted.

"I participated in their meditations and in doing so I had flashbacks to other lifetimes spent in such temples in India, Thailand, Japan and Korea. I remembered how in the old days, the martial arts were practiced in combination with meditation and a life in solitude. Martial arts were the vehicles through which the spirit was conveyed. The spirit was strengthened in meditation: the body was educated in the physical strength and skills of combat. It is no coincidence that the emperors and their ministers handpicked the best warriors from the temples with the highest disciplines. These men had proven themselves of loyalty, commitment and above all self control over their desires and physical needs."

For Ingrid, meditation meant a reuniting with her own soul and becoming aware of her own timeless nature.

She explains that this method lays the foundation for a successful physical condition favoring alertness and ever-present awareness necessary in martial arts. To her, martial arts meant a state of mind, not a mere means of self defense.

After three weeks, she returned to Tokyo with a new grasp of Japanese language skills.

The language entered her blood as had everything else about Japan. She felt like a sponge, soaking up the vibes around her. She was thrilled with the orderliness of Japanese life, the politeness and traditional values and the predictable behavior of the locals.

CHAPTER 7

ENLIGHTEN ME, ASIA!

Now it was time to visit Korea. Ever since taking up Tae Kwon Do, Ingrid Vallieres had become convinced that the Korean mentality was the strongest among the Asian people.

"I found all Korean martial arts teachers extremely dedicated, devoted to what they were doing and strong-minded," she says. "There never seemed to be a halfhearted, weak personality among them but rather showed strong determination in their actions. This always deeply impressed me."

Tae Kwon Do is the Korean traditional martial art. It includes mainly footwork and high flying kicks and it allows you to attack or defend yourself from a distance, unlike Judo. In Judo, you must be close to a person in order to grab him.

Ingrid says she picked Tae Kwon Do to master because she was fascinated by the jumping and flying kicks.

"Of all the martial arts this is the least attached to the ground. It allows you to get up in the air. For me, it was reminiscent of both my life as a Samurai and a second in which I was a female warrior. In that life I was born into an oppressed people who were ruled and oppressed by a Chinese feudal system."

One of her main goals in visiting Korea was to visit the martial arts gyms and to meet more people who lived and represented this spirit.

She remembers that her first impression of Seoul was of a large bustling city. It was less clean and less organized than Tokyo, and its people were tougher than the Japanese and not as polite. There, she soon learned you had to take care of yourself and not expect others to help you. Adjustment to this culture was rather difficult, as she had been spoiled by the well-behaved Japanese and somehow had expected Korea to be similar.

Mr. Kim, her Tae Kwon Do Master in Germany, had given her the address of his sister, and Ingrid stayed with her for several days and was integrated into the Korean family lifestyle.

While in Seoul, she visited the Tae Kwon Do Association headquarters. She was shown around several of the universities as well as the center where masters are educated before they are sent abroad to teach the martial art.

"It was a delight for me to be right at the heart of the Tae Kwon Do Federation where this martial arts technique was constantly studied and improved. Today this form of martial arts can be found in competition at the Olympics as well as around the world."

In 1972, Seoul had a 10:00 p.m. curfew because of tensions with North Korea. By 8:00 p.m. there would be a lot of turmoil in the streets as everyone dashed around finding the right bus on which to ride home. If you didn't make it home by curfew, you had to find a nightclub in which to stay until the next morning when the curfew lifted. If you were caught out on the street after curfew, you would be arrested.

"And the Koreans could surprise you. One day, I was walking through the city and became lost. I stopped a man and asked him directions. After a few moments of conversation, he suddenly stopped and bowed to me."

Ingrid stared at him in confusion.

"One moment, dear lady," he said as he disappeared into a nearby department store.

She stood there for several minutes feeling a little confused and uncertain about what to do next. As suddenly as he disappeared the man reappeared, carrying a huge Korean doll in a glass case.

"This is for you, dear lady," he said as he held it out to her.

"Oh, but I can't accept this," Ingrid stammered.

"Please. It is my greatest pleasure to give to one so beautiful," he pleaded.

"I felt strange and embarrassed, standing there in the street and being offered this very precious gift, but I felt it would have been impolite and rude not to accept it. I thanked him, and he walked away.

I never saw this man again. He never asked my address or if he could meet me somewhere. He simply appeared, gave me this beautiful gift and then disappeared out of my life."

This surprise gifting to her by Asian men happened quite often on her trip. None of them ever asked anything of her but to be allowed to bestow their presents. They would then turn around and walk away.

A few days after the doll incident, Ingrid left Seoul and headed south to Pusan. On her way south, she visited the countryside.

"Although most of the Koreans don't speak English or German, the older people who lived through the Japanese-Korean War do know some Japanese, so we communicated quite well."

While Korea turned out to be all she'd hoped for in its culture and martial arts, she realized that this country wouldn't be a place she would want to live. Life seemed more strenuous in that divided country than it did in Japan.

At Pusan, the southernmost city in Korea, she took the ferry to Shimonoseki, a Japanese harbor city that lies at the southern tip of the island, Kyushu.

"I was standing at the rail, staring at the fading Korean shore when I was startled by a voice behind me," Ingrid recounts.

"Hi there, gorgeous," a male voice said.

She whirled around and stared into the bluest eyes she'd ever seen. "I beg your pardon?"

"Hi, I'm Allan."

He appeared a little older than Ingrid, with tousled brown hair and a great smile. From the look of his clothes she guessed he was an American.

"Hello. My name is Ingrid."

It turned out he was an American, just as Ingrid thought, and he was also traveling alone. "I'm going to hitchhike to Tokyo," he said sometime later. "Want to go with me?"

"Why not?" she said without a moment's hesitation. "I've never hitchhiked before, but with such a tall, strong man coming along, it might be interesting."

"We can stop in youth hostels along the way," he said.

"My plan exactly." Ingrid beamed at him. This was going to be fun!

They soon found out that people didn't hitchhike in Japan. When Allan stuck out his thumb, the drivers would stop and ask if they were in trouble and needed help. When they explained they wanted to go to the next city, some of the drivers took them there as a courtesy, even when it was out of their way.

By the end of their first day on the road, they had made some headway getting to Tokyo, , and they found beds in a youth hostel. That night, Ingrid had a hard time falling asleep. She knew that once she arrived back in Tokyo, she would have to return to her job in Germany. Her three and a half month vacation was coming to a fast end, and her company was expecting her to return. But she didn't want to leave this wonderful country. What to do? Breaking business contracts was an unthinkable issue for her, and she did have a contract with them. On the other hand, every cell of her body cried out to stay in Japan.

"While I was a loyal person and did not like the idea of having been granted the generous leave only to break my contract, I rationalized privately that my reasons for returning home - my job, family matters and friends - were not really a calling such as I was now experiencing.

How could I leave Japan? I loved it so, through the half-remembered memories of other lives, other times in this enchanting place," says Ingrid.

She tossed and turned in her bed, as thoughts and feelings churned over and over in her mind until the room lightened with the early promise of dawn. Finally, she arose and walked to the window quietly so as not to disturb the other members of the youth hostel who were still asleep.

Standing there, watching the sky grow rosy in the dawn, something inside her demanded STAY! You may never get another chance like this. This is the time. This country is good to you and you feel exhilarated and happy being here. If you return to this country a few years from now, maybe all those good opportunities you have now will not be there.

Later that morning Ingrid wrote her employer and resigned her position. She wrote she was sorry, but she would not return because the current situation was too important to her.

She left the youth hostel with an easy mind, knowing she had made the right choice. It took all her courage to give up the beginning of a promising career to take an uncertain path with an uncertain outcome.

It was one of the most important decisions of her life. This would become a philosophy of hers which she applied in her later therapeutical work:

She formulated her philosophy as "Follow your heart no matter what the outer circumstances may be."

CHAPTER 8

THE GERMAN GEISHA

It took Allan and Ingrid three days to hitchhike back to Tokyo. The last part of the trip was by truck. By then it was mid-June, 1972. The young travelers parted as casually as they met. It had been an interesting adventure, but Ingrid was anxious to move on.

With no specific place to go, she found a USO in the downtown Tokyo's Ginza, a service facility for American soldiers which served food and drink and was open to the public. She found it to be a comfortable place to read and linger.

She entered and took a place at the counter. After she ordered a meal, an Australian named John sat down next to her. Soon they were deep in conversation. He was a teacher who gave private English lessons and lived in Tokyo. He showed her the want ad section in the newspaper where there were a number of requests for English teachers to work privately and for companies.

When Ingrid explained her situation to him – no place to stay and no job yet - John spontaneously offered her his apartment for two weeks while he traveled to Korea.

While at the USO, she called some of the want ads for English teachers and made appointments to be interviewed. John and she then went to his one room apartment where he showed her how to turn on the Japanese stove and other appliances that were foreign to her.

She stayed in a youth hostel for a couple of days until he left.

Over the next several days, she interviewed as an English and German teacher with Japanese firms and private students. It was helpful that Ingrid has very little German accent when speaking English.

"I suppose that's because of those several years I spent as a child in America where I attended grade school. The English knowledge of the Japanese was so low anyway that they would not be able to detect a difference between my style of English and the American accents," she says.

Everything in her personal life now began to develop very fast, almost as if there were some kind of divine plan that she should stay in Japan. She met a young Australian couple who were John's friends. They, too, had an upcoming trip planned to Korea. They would be gone for two months, so they offered to let her stay at their apartment while they were away. She found it an easy transition from John's place to theirs, and gave her enough time to get work and find a place of her own.

In Japan, apartments are very scarce, extremely small and outrageously expensive. The less expensive ones are situated far outside Tokyo. So Ingrid marvels even today at her luck that the two apartments became available when she needed them.

"It was as though they were heaven-sent. It appeared to me that my decision to stay was correct. The Australian woman and I would become good friends."

"Have you ever thought of taking a job in one of the nightclubs?" she asked Ingrid one day.

"Are you serious?" Ingrid said.

"Well, it turned out that this woman was not only a teacher, but she also worked in one of the Japanese nightclubs where she made very good money. She explained how innocent the Japanese nightclubs were and how you only sat with customers, had drinks and talked with them.

I was curious, so she took me along one evening to the nightclub in Shinjuku where she worked."

Ingrid remembers the club as having many small tables and a stage where performers would sing and dance. Her friend introduced her to the manager who smiled at her and said in Japanese "Bijin desu ne-wakarimasu ka? You are very pretty, do you understand?

He hired her immediately. That was her first night job as a hostess. She had to buy a few pretty dresses to work there. It was, she remembers, an easy job. The customers arrived and sat at a table. The manager would assign several girls to them. There was never a question that the customers would not accept the hostesses which meant that they had to pay extra charges for the girls and for their drinks.

In Germany, such a job would automatically imply that the girls were low class and the interaction between customers and hostesses would be mainly geared toward sexual encounters. In Japan, on the other hand, the conversations between customers and hostesses was very light, very intellectual or very political or just funny, depending on the club and the area it was situated.

Shinjuku was the place for the young crowd, so the customers were very young and did not look for intellectual conversations as compared to high-class areas like the Ginza. So it was very entertaining for her to speak to young Japanese, and, since they spoke hardly any English, she was forced to understand and speak Japanese more and more fluently. The mixture of Japanese and foreign hostesses was approximately 50-50. The girls were paid about 8000 Yen a night, roughly $40 in American money which was, at that time an excellent income for a fun and easy job.

Ingrid notes that Japanese people appeared to be drawn to her from the first days she entered the country. She liked them and they her. In the club, she realized she had an enormous effect on Japanese men.

Since Japanese people are somewhat shy and do not show affection openly, they need an outer event as an excuse to get closer to others.

"I assume that is why the nightclub business in Japan is so vital and plays such an important part in the lives of Japanese people. In the clubs, they lose this traditional distance to each other and the stiff ways of communication loosen up. For instance, it is impossible for a Japanese to just speak to their countrymen and women, because the language contains many different levels of politeness. If you do not know the rank and position of the other person, you don't know which level of speech to choose."

She explains that is the reason Japanese always exchange their business cards first. That way, they get this uncertainty out of the way so they can be formally introduced properly to private and business contacts.

Japanese daily life is usually stiff and full of conventions, must-do's, and its people are performance-driven. The only way they can loosen up is in the nightlife in which clubs play an enormous role.

After a few weeks on her new job, Ingrid says her looks seemed to change. She became more feminine and pretty. Her hair and skin appeared very beautiful, and she dressed more elegantly than before.

Since her childhood, she had dreamed of having black hair and brown eyes. But now, she became at peace with her looks - medium blonde hair and blue eyes - because these were the features the Japanese admired very much.

Unlike India and Thailand, where women did not dye their hair, Japanese women often dyed their hair brown or auburn in imitation of the Western look.

Ingrid felt very special and very desirable. In the club, she was told many times that she was very pretty, gentle and smart, because she caught onto the Japanese language in so little time. She hadn't worked in the club a week before she knew intuitively that she would soon meet a Japanese man who would become her lover and that she would move in with him.

Several days later, she was approached by two "scouts" or hostess headhunters, who were introduced to her by another hostess. They offered her a job in Ginza, the first-class and most expensive nightlife area.

During the day, she taught English and German privately to various students. Most of them were adults trying hard to learn the various languages. She was surprised how little English these people knew in spite of their years of English language classes.

At night, she was a popular nightclub hostess. Her new club at Ginza was much more lavish than her first employment. It was furnished in white leather. The hostesses wore expensive long evening gowns or dressed as Geishas in kimonos and fancy hairstyles. The customers were older and were managers and executives of companies. The entertainment was subdued, consisting of a singer and a pianist.

Her salary doubled, which she says was a blessing since she had to buy new gowns such as the others wore. She remembers that this club was the place where she learned the most about Japanese corporate life and about the relationships between people.

Again, she was very popular because she caught quickly onto the Japanese mentality and adapted to it.

"You are not at all like a foreigner. You are like Japanese!" she was told over and over again. They also commented about her long legs. "Where did you get those gorgeous legs?" she would be asked.

"Japanese women have short legs, and so when we sat together, the length of my legs was even more pronounced. I am 5'8", much taller than the Japanese women," she says.

She got to know the hostesses because they talked openly about themselves and their lifestyles. She also got along well with the manager and waiters. It was, she recalls, all like a big family.

"The Japanese do not gossip or talk bad behind each other's back. The girls were not jealous of each other as to who looked better or made more money. Instead, they helped and supported each other wherever possible. Once, another hostess bought a dark blue velvet dress, exactly like one I had already worn to the club. This was considered bad taste and poor observation for her to buy the same exact dress as mine."

The other girls commented: "me ga warui? She has bad eyesight. Too bad, isn't it?" The politeness prevailed.

Even the customers behaved well. The club was tremendously overpriced. It cost the customers approximately $1,000 to $2,000 to come to it, but from the hostesses they only expected conversation and to be looked after when they wanted drinks.

The formality and discipline were so strong that even a "dead-drunk" customer never lost his containment or used bad or dirty language. They would just become quiet or funny or talk nonsense. They were never insulting or fresh with anyone.

Ingrid met interesting people and led many interesting and intellectual discussions about such topics as the different countries, lifestyles, politics and economics. Some customers invited the girls out to eat. Again, this was a totally innocent affair where usually several girls would join. Club life was the substitute for private relationships.

She then took on a second club job after midnight, since the work paid well and her day teaching job didn't start until afternoon. Ingrid has never needed a lot of sleep, and she thrived on this routine. This new club, in Roppongi, offered a live band instead of one pianist, and it was a much livelier place than where she worked earlier in the evening.

CHAPTER 9

LOVE AND TRAGEDY

Remember Ingrid's prophecy that soon she would find a Japanese lover? One night she looked up and there he was - Makoto.

"I saw this Japanese man sitting at another table, looking at me and laughing. He finally requested that I sit with him," she says.

Makoto looked quite different from the others, because he was tall and had a Mongolian look to him. He didn't speak English, so he and Ingrid spoke together in Japanese about various things. In the nights that followed, he kept coming back to see her. They began dating and before long they were in love.

"My two-month apartment lease with the Australian couple was up, so I filed an application with an agent to find my own apartment. Makoto volunteered to assist in the apartment hunt," she says.

"This is silly," he told her one day, "Why don't you just move in with me?" The future she had envisioned was coming true.

"I said 'Yes, darling,' very quickly."

She moved in with Makoto and soon he proposed marriage.

"Makoto encouraged me to start a modeling career and soon I began modeling for advertising and fashion print jobs in magazines. Once I modeled a red velvet German folkloristic dress on Japanese television. I started to dress very stylishly, like a professional model, and I wore lots of big hats. To my delight, I was often asked if I were a model, which of course I was."

A manager of a German promotion board offered her a job as hostess for German products in the large Tokyo department stores. Now, she had four different kinds of jobs and enjoyed every one of them.

"Sometimes I was busy 24 hours around the clock. Soon I was also employed giving German lessons to the Japanese employees of a large German-owned company."

Ingrid found Makoto's lifestyle entirely to her liking. He was, she says, very classy. "Many women envied me. He was different from the typical Japanese man insofar as he didn't follow the crowd. He was very social. We went on numerous short trips together. In short, life was perfect for me. I had created my own lifestyle. It was not necessarily the constrictive Japanese lifestyle but rather that of a foreigner living in Japan with all the freedom to do as one pleases."

She explains that the Japanese lifestyle, on the other hand, is very much by rote, with the company dictating your activities from vacations to education to even dating and matrimony.

There, the company chooses you rather than you choosing the company for which to work. "Now I was becoming more aware of the downside of Japanese life, including the rigid types of conversations and lifestyles. Certain things were to be said both at various occasions and when things were to be done - nothing else. Even conversations were predictable and stereotyped. Within my realm of work, I luckily had the opportunity to know the people on a more personal level; otherwise it would have been very difficult to get closer to them. But, all in all, it was one of the most exciting years of my life. Of course it couldn't last. Life had other things in mind for me," she says.

She woke up early the morning of April 8, 1973. It was cold, and she shivered as she turned on the gas stove to heat the room.

Suddenly, the stove exploded in her face.

"I remember seeing my pajamas catch fire, as I screamed and fell on the floor. The flames were so intense and it happened so fast that I couldn't get my clothes off. Flashes of my present life came and went in front of my eyes. It seemed as if my spirit was struggling to free itself of my body. I wanted my parents."

"Ingrid, my God," she heard Makoto scream somewhere far away and realized he was beating out the flames with blankets. She remembers it seemed as if it were happening to someone else.

Soon the medics arrived and she was taken by ambulance to the hospital.

"I was jolted back again into this present life. At the hospital, I was put in an oxygen tent.

Bandages were wrapped around my body; my swollen head was covered with a violet-colored medicine."

"I'm so stiff," she would moan to Makoto, "I can't move." "But you're alive," he would reassure her.

"Alive? Barely. Daily I seemed to lose more and more contact with my body and my present life as Ingrid. As I lay there in pain, I seemed to remember other lives filled with burning machinery, being burned alive at the stake and even dying of natural catastrophes. I knew that this kind of injury had happened to me under different circumstances in past lives."

She remembers coming to the point of death in that Tokyo hospital. It was as if she were at some great crossroads, and her spirit yearned to be free of the suffering body.

She found herself on the spiritual plane where there was no more pain or suffering, just awareness of being light, transparent and floating. It was tempting, she admits, to stay there.

"As I contemplated my death, an inner voice said 'NO, I want to live!'"

She knew there was something left to do. It wasn't her time to die, and, she decided, it would be a shame to waste the experiences and knowledge already gained in the 20 years of her present life. She decided that if there were something she was to do in this life, it would be better to do it this time rather than carry it over to her next life.

"I'd led an interesting and bold lifestyle, had met unusual people and had tapped into the deep sources of spiritual knowledge. With death, I knew I would only have to go back through birth again, go through schooling again, so much trouble to regain all that I had now. So, considering 'karmic economics', I decided that I was not going to start all over again but to stay with the body I had. I would recover and build on the experience gathered so far."

The same voice told her she had not yet completed her mission for this lifetime. "Completed IT? I didn't even know what IT was. Somehow, I knew it would be revealed to me in good time."

When Ingrid helps others regress into their past lives, she always tells them that you must be willing to work with the unknown before you start. Once you open yourself up to the development of your soul, you must be willing to pay the price. That price may be giving up a comfortable state of mind, unreal assumptions or even ingrained habits.

Whenever you open yourself up to change, as Ingrid was about to do, some things that are not for our higher good will be taken away, but the important thing is that we gain the truth which becomes part of our timeless soul.

"Looking back at this time, I now realize this near death experience was crucial in my becoming a past life therapist and in how I would come to define myself.

"There is a simple truth: you must accept challenges when they arise. Don't put them off, because they will become harder, the longer you procrastinate.

"The moment I decided to repossess this life, my body came back to me. I knew I had to awaken from my delirium, get my body healed and fill it again with energy. It would be a strenuous and painful process," she remembers.

"The treatment in the Tokyo hospital was old fashioned and very painful. Every day, the bandages were taken off and the gauze scrubbed off in an oxygen bubble bath. It was horrible, and I screamed in agony as they rubbed my raw flesh. I had sustained first, second and third degree burns. Afterwards, ointment and bandages were reapplied.

"I dreaded the morning ritual. I was probably the only patient in the hospital who screamed during treatment: the Japanese never scream but bear their pain in silence."

Makoto had called the German Embassy shortly after Ingrid's accident. An Embassy official paid her a visit in the hospital, and she asked him to inform her parents in Germany about her condition and what had happened to her.

One afternoon, about two weeks after Ingrid entered the hospital, the room door opened.

Her mother was standing there.

"Oh, Mama, you came!" moaned the bandaged figure on the bed.

"Of course. Did you ever think I wouldn't?" her mother asked, with tears in her eyes.

Ingrid felt tears burning hot against her eyelids. Her face was the only part of her body not wrapped in gauze.

"I'm so glad you're here," she said between sobs.

Ingrid, always the optimist, had never dreamed she would find herself in this condition, barely back from the brink of death.

"It's going to be all right, darling," her mother said through her own tears.

She was horrified to learn the extent and the seriousness of her daughter's injuries, and Ingrid, seeing her mother there felt as if a great weight had lifted off her.

"I wouldn't be able to eat solid food for another week, and was still fed through infusions. With Mama there, I got a big boost of encouragement in my fight for survival. In this hospital, patients received only medical treatment. Food and other needs were your responsibility. Mama saw to those needs in the days and weeks ahead," she says remembering those terrible days.

"Will I ever walk again, doctor?" Ingrid asked one day. "My body is so stiff, I can't move it."

He told her that this was just her body in shock reacting to the burns. Shortly after that, she was encouraged to get out of bed and walk. At first, it seemed impossible to the young burn victim, but she found that as the days went by it became easier and easier. Soon, all she had left to deal with was cosmetic surgery. There had been no serious damage to her health or her mobility.

"I felt I had been granted a second chance at life. I determined that from now on I would appreciate life even more than before. Every new day was a gift. Now it was time to digest what I had learned and to make something useful of it."

There is an old Chinese saying which Ingrid firmly believes: "if a mishap occurs in your life, wait two years and it will turn into good luck."

She explains that in both our present and our past lives, if we can understand our past misfortunes, they will ultimately turn into good fortunes. What we learn from our unhappy experiences, if we look at them in a positive light, will help us in the end and more than pay for that initial loss. And so it would prove to be with her own misadventure.

CHAPTER 10

THE PATH BECOMES CLEAR

"After five weeks of treatment in the Tokyo hospital, Mama brought me home to Germany where I underwent massive plastic surgery. I did not want this done in Japan, and my German medical insurance covered this treatment," she says.

Her trip by ambulance to the airport was her first trip out of the hospital. It was a strange feeling, leaving Japan in this manner. She wondered when she would come back. Somehow, she knew that someday she would.

"I thought I would never see my Japanese lover Makoto again after he said goodbye to me the day I left his country, but he came to visit me in Germany a year or so after I left Japan. I was in the middle of having necessary plastic surgeries done at the time. It was an awkward meeting. My life in Japan was so different, colorful, entertaining, but now in Germany I was in a recovery mode.

Although our relationship was still strong during that visit, we did not make any plans for the future. Several years later, when I was 23, I visited him in Los Angeles where he had moved. We met for a weekend to celebrate the good old times. After that, I never saw him again, I tried to find his address in Japan but this is almost an impossible task. Because of the Japanese characters, words can be pronounced in different ways, and people not directly related have no right to inquire addresses of the proper city halls."

But all that was before her. It was a very injured Ingrid who left Japan and returned to Stuttgart to face lengthy rehabilitation and plastic surgery.

When her plane touched down in Stuttgart, another ambulance was waiting to meet her and to deliver her to a local hospital where she was extensively examined for the planned plastic surgery.

"Every day, a physiotherapist came into my hospital room. We did hand stretching exercises, as my hands had become very stiff because of my burns. When I bent them, my skin cracked open, causing them to bleed. It was very painful."

She has never forgotten her therapist's words.

"If you want to become an invalid, you only have to omit your exercises for one day," she said.

Although Ingrid thought this a bold and tough statement, she says that it helped her see the reason for the painful ordeal and to persist through it.

"Unfortunately, the plastic surgery offered by this hospital proved not to be very good. Worse still, they offered recommendations for care which only worsened the condition of my skin.

"I decided to find a specialist. This was not an easy task, because good plastic surgeons were sought after by celebrities and had no openings for years. One specialized clinic recommended that I come in several times during two years. This would have meant that I could not work and would always be on call, having surgery, recovering, going back again to the clinic to repeat the whole routine over and over. I was eager to return to the active world, but my physical condition was such that my skin grafts burned or tingled and I had trouble moving my head and hands. Due to my skin's sensitivity, I couldn't wear tight or thick clothing, nor could I bear extreme heat or cold.

"Fortunately, I found a private clinic that had recently opened in Bavaria. The head plastic surgeon was a very kind, professional and understanding man. He explained exactly what needed to be done, and he agreed to carry out several operations within a few weeks.

Then I had a year's time before the next series of surgeries. Today, very little of the scarring remains, thanks to the skill of my surgeon."

While Ingrid lay recuperating and wondering exactly why she had returned to this life, her old friend Roland visited her. What he told her changed her life.

"I've had a past life regression," Roland said. "You did what?" she asked in fascination.

"Yes, I went back into my past lives and it was the most fascinating experience," he said enthusiastically.

"Oh? So who were you?"

"One time, I was a pirate and another time I was a monk," he said. "You must try it, Ingrid!"

Going on to explain that past life regression is not just a philosophy but something to know, he said he was now taking classes in this exciting new approach.

"And Roland was a fast friend during all this time of my troubles. It is an old saying that it is in distressful times you know your true friends. And not many of my former friends were around to support me at this stage. Some words of encouragement, going out on a walk, seeing a movie - little things like those made life worthwhile during those dark days of recuperation. And Roland never failed to be there when I needed him."

Her recent plastic surgery now behind her, Ingrid was finally free to find a job. Roland used his connection to a local hospital to help her get on as a part time secretary there.

"And it would be Roland," she says, "who led me, perhaps inadvertently, to my life's purpose."

CHAPTER 11

THE ANSWERS LIE IN OUR PAST

"I had made such great plans that year in Japan before the accident," says Ingrid. "I was going to open a business there so I could work on the earthly plane. It had seemed the right thing to do, considering my good fortune there. It now became obvious to me that this was not what I was supposed to do in this life. In spite of all my meditation and spiritual exercises, I was now suffering from a lack of self-confidence, from melancholy and varying moods. Inner stability was lacking and something was preventing me from living and developing my personality to the fullest."

Maybe the answer lay in her past. Roland had reminded her that it was not necessarily her past in this life, but it could lay in other lives she had led as well. Could this be true? Ingrid began to wonder.

"Roland's excursion into his own past lives now encouraged me to do likewise. After all, hadn't I experienced strange memories of living in other countries and other times already?" Her first venture into reincarnation was through Dianetics. There, she learned how they taught regression. According to this belief, the subconscious mind stores all past incidents and by way of the "time track" you can move backward to access certain experiences.

Something else happened during her short stay with Dianetics: she fell in love with and married Marc, a handsome young French Canadian who, at 20, was a few years younger than her. While living in Canada, he had started studying the theories by Dianetics founder L. Ron Hubbard about the metaphysical relationship between mind and body and had come to Germany to further his education. He and Ingrid met when they both attended a study course. They were immediately attracted to each other.

"I suppose in retrospect, much of the attraction was the fact that we were both starting out on our studies of Dianetics and had many of the same interests and continued with our explorations in this philosophy. During my first regressions with this method, I found I had a lifetime as: a Spanish woman who lived a poor, miserable life in a desert like area.

"In this time, approximately 700 years ago, poverty reigned. I did not have much food to cook or eat much less to save for another day. I lived in an area that was always hot, sandy and dry where I raised hell with my husband who never brought back food or money. It was a. desperate life; but now I know that it wasn't all his fault. When I saw that lifetime, I had to chuckle since this was my anti-type of my present incarnation. In my present life, I hardly ever argue and definitely would find fault with people who worsen the current situation by antagonizing and emotionalizing with others.

"In those early regressions of mine, I found another one lived in the Middle East as a soldier. And I remembered that I was a Japanese Geisha in another one. There was even one where I was a man who lived in and roamed the mountains with a panther as his best friend. There were many others, as well.

"From my studies in Dianetics, I learned that the mind works on the basis of hypnosis and creates patterns that can last many lifetimes. The subconscious is the basic instinct with all life forms. Should there be a threat to an organism's life, this traumatic event is stored within the subconscious. If a similar perception of a threat should occur, whether in the same or a future life, the subconscious will emit warning signals to tell the entity to feel fear, attempt avoidance or escape the situation.

"I also learned that the purpose of the subconscious is to aid the survival and safety of the organism. This it does by trying to help it avoid the behaviors and surroundings that are dangerous, on the one hand, while, on the other, to choose behaviors or surroundings that are favorable."

Before long, she had explored the subject of Dianetics in depth and was ready to move on.

"With Dianetics, it seemed we were only touching on our past lives, rather like looking at pictures, but we were not studying these lives in any depth. I resolved to further my studies elsewhere with other people. I felt there was more to be learned."

Marc, however, was firmly attached to their present program.

"The impact of Dianetics is very strong, and he wanted to continue with it, while I was ready to move ahead with my life. It was an amicable separation. I wasn't really into getting a divorce at the time, as I certainly had no intentions of remarrying any time soon.

"Several years later, in 1983, he contacted my parents for my current address and sent me a letter asking for a divorce. It seemed he wanted to remarry. I agreed to do so. When the divorce papers came, I signed them, sent them back, and that was that. I was again totally free to be me. I understand Marc stayed with Dianetics, although I have never seen him since. I did, however, visit his parents during one of my seminar engagements in Canada."

By the time Ingrid and Marc separated, she was writing the first of her five published books and was starting to give professional consultations in her practice. She was now also giving lectures and seminars around Europe. Because there were very few past life therapists who specialized in the field in those days, she became one of the pioneers in this type of work.

"But that was all ahead of me when I left Marc in 1976," says Ingrid. "I wanted to study with Dr. Morris Netherton, a man who was just starting to become an authority in the field of past life regression. I called him at his home in Los Angeles, and he invited me to come and learn from him. Immediately, I flew to Los Angeles to begin my new training."

She had no idea what Los Angeles would be like. She supposed that it might be a little like New York City, which she had visited before.

"Wrong! Instead of a condensed city, I discovered one that spread out for miles in all directions. Unlike our European cities, Los Angeles doesn't seem to really have a main core. Since public transportation is impossible there, I always rented a car during my stays there. I came to Los Angeles during the spring, when California's weather is at its best, neither too warm nor too cold."

She met Dr. Netherton for the first time in his office. He was younger than she expected.

She judged him to be about ten years older than she was. She found he had a very practical, modern and straightforward approach to past life regression. A psychologist rather than a metaphysicist, the doctor fell into this field through his work as a co-therapist. He told Ingrid it had only been a fascinating experiment at first, but he became a believer in reincarnation as these experiments progressed.

"I never had a belief attached to it," he told her.

"I was one of a small number of students that first time," says Ingrid. "It was more of an interest group than a formal schooling. Later, as more students flocked to him, the interest group grew into structured, professional classes. What we had started with our little group was the beginning of formalized studies in past life therapy.

"I studied with him, off and on, for two and a half years. The main thing I learned from him was to ask straight, simple questions of my clients rather than the pre-set procedures followed by Dianetics. While they only ask questions through a written procedure, never deviating from these, Dr. Netherton's work was different. Under his technique, the analyst could ask questions and probe into the client's stories. This helped the clients relive the incidents and know their past lives in detail rather than only glimpse a picture of the past life. By reliving and learning from the experience, it released any negative content."

A few years later Dr. Netherton visited Ingrid in Germany and gave many professional training seminars to the European audiences. By that time, reincarnation was becoming a hot topic in Europe.

Ingrid says that her experience has been that ninety five percent of her clients need this thorough probing to get them through the past life experience and to learn the needed lessons from it. When that happens, you can let go of the trauma associated with that past life experience.

"The difference between our present and our past lives is that in this lifetime we have yet to experience death. We have emotional incidents, but our deep traumas come from those past lives that ended in violent death. This trauma can be triggered by our encountering a similar incident to one in our past.

"The odd thing about my later successes in this field was that actually, after I finished my studies in 1978 with Dr. Netherton, I hadn't any plans to set up a practice of my own. I thought of my studies as a hobby, not a profession in which I could make a living."

Ingrid returned to Germany, her studies concluded, to find that reincarnation was becoming a hot topic. A German author, Thorwald Dethlefsen had just published a book about how hypnosis could be used to induce past life regression.

CHAPTER 12

PIONEERING IN PAST LIFE THERAPY

"When I returned home to Stuttgart not having a clue as to what I would do next with my life. I stayed a few weeks with my parents, while I cast about for a plan," says Ingrid.

She took a job as a temporary foreign language secretary. Sometime around her fifth week doing this, it suddenly dawned on her that, if the temp service could hire her out and keep a large share of money paid out by firms, why couldn't she hire herself out? She could become her own translation company and would be free to come and go as she pleased.

"I called a CPA to find out what such a project would entail. After he told me, he asked if I were available for a temp position in his company, and I said I was. He asked me - over the phone - if I could start work immediately. I had my first contract, as if handed to me on a silver platter."

To Ingrid's delight, her business continued to grow. The work came to her.

"I stayed a very long time with an American sewing machine company's German plant, replacing one of their secretaries who was going on vacation. The secretary never did come back to work, so I stayed at that job until they found a replacement."

Immediately at the end of that job, she was offered another temp job by the same company. This time it was for a secretary going on maternity leave. That company kept me so busy, I never needed to seek another client. I was not an employee but an associate and worked very hard for them, in spite of my temp status."

In the meantime, Ingrid, with her knowledge of past life regression learned through her years of studies in the United States, discovered a new line of work.

"My friends knew about this training, and past life regressions were a new fad. They asked me to give them regressions, so I did this on the side. My client list finally grew so large; I decided I couldn't do it for free anymore. I formed my second company, The Institute for Past Life Research. This Institute quickly attracted people who wanted to find out about their past."

One of her early clients was a young man, Fritz. His story is, she says, an excellent example of how powerful our past lives are on our present. They are powerful, because they include our unfinished business.

This was true about Fritz. He came to Ingrid with a very strange problem. Not only did he have a strong compulsion to wash himself. He told her that sometimes he felt as if his mouth was full of what seemed to be feathers and he had to spit them out. Another recurring plight was that he felt unbearably warm at times.

He explained to her that the compulsions began when he was a trainee for an optometrist. Working with him was a young woman trainee. His strange travail began one day when she passed him a tool.

"Suddenly, I felt as though I had to go and immediately wash that tool," he said.

"Soon it got worse. Not only did I have to wash the tool, but I had to wash myself over and over again, until finally I couldn't leave my home. I couldn't even look at a picture of a pair of glasses without them reminding me of her and then I would have to go wash myself again."

What an interesting case, Ingrid thought. She knew he wasn't psychotic, but he was rather a man who had lost control of his life.

Perhaps she could help him. After she did several regressions, his story and the cause of his fixations began to emerge.

"Where are you now?" Ingrid asked him during this regression.

"I'm a stableman and I'm in charge of m'lady's horses," he said.

He explained that he saw himself as a young, hard working man who is very loyal to his employer, a very strict woman.

"A storm is building up fast," he continued.

His voice suddenly changed to one of horror. "Oh, no! The horses have gotten loose in the storm. M'lady is furious with me. No, no. Oh, God, she's ordered me tarred and feathered. There are people watching. I feel so ashamed. Now they're bringing in the tar. I can smell it.

"A housemaid brings a sackful of feathers. Everyone is laughing. They pour the tar over me. Oh no, it burns so bad. Now they're dumping the feathers. Some are in my mouth. I'm choking on them. My skin! I've got to get the tar off my skin! I wash and wash, but it won't come off."

This experience impaired him for the rest of that life. When his regression period ended, he realized that the young woman trainee had been "m'lady" in that other, long ago life. Fritz's wash compulsion stopped at that moment. A few weeks later, he came back to tell me he was totally cured. He had even been able to leave his house to go to his aunt's funeral.

Interestingly, his case was a true example of the law of Karma, that what you do in one life, you will be paid back for in another.

Fritz continued with his regressions. He learned that where in his life as a stableman, he was the victim. In another lifetime he had been the victimizer as an American Indian.

"The village is under attack. I've got to get away," he remembered.

He ran away, but he left his family and his village to their fate. This also explained an ongoing troubles with relationships to women and with authority in general.

Fritz was delighted with his successful regressions. Now cured of his wash compulsion, he referred many of his friends to Ingrid.

"Unfortunately, since they were all compulsion cases, I couldn't help some of them.

"It depends on the attitude of the patient. How high is your responsibility level, including the responsibility to change your life? You can only get out of therapy what you are willing to put in it. Pursuing past life therapy is very responsible work."

She points out that Fritz was willing to try to find the cause of his obsessions. Others, she regrets to say, were not. He and Ingrid remain in contact to this day. Happily over his former obsessions, including trouble with women, he's now married. He and his wife have two beautiful children. He is doing very well in this life, and Ingrid says she is happy for him.

Fritz came to her in 1979, a year that would prove to be a busy one for Ingrid Valieres.

That her own spiritual path had suddenly become a practical profession astounded her more than anyone else.

"I have always been fascinated with the workings of the mind. Philosophy and religion, I engaged in as an auto-didact, in that I was for the most part self-taught. Psychology as it was taught at university did not capture me. And Science has not been very successful when it comes to exploring and explaining mental phenomena. As in many forms of alternative medicines, there exists non-scientific knowledge of many topics which much later is confirmed by "science."

"We know that inventions are discovered at several locations at the same time. They have always been there, but nobody had discovered them before. So, there seems to be an expecting attitude of the person searching, as well as a receptiveness of the times and the people to allow a breakthrough in the invention to occur at such a time. This seems true of the growing interest in past life regression therapy in Western countries. The East has long held a strong belief in reincarnation."

Some of Ingrid's new clients would come to her as unbelievers and become believers, as their pasts were laid out for them. Others were already convinced that past lives were a logical explanation for so many phenomena and wanted to learn all about them. Her old friend Roland, although he was now into Yoga and memorization, helped Ingrid out by sending her new clients and setting up seminars for her.

"As my practice built, I enrolled in the German Alternative Medicine School. This allowed me to become a legally licensed therapist. It took me two years as a part-time student to learn about legal ramifications of treating patients with illnesses. I learned to diagnose major illnesses and I studied such alternative healing methods as homeopathy, herbal treatments and natural remedies."

Ingrid likes to point out that since we have all been victims and victimizers at various times in our past lives, it is necessary in curing trauma to find both when you were the victim and when you were the victimizer. In Karma, we suffer if we do harm to another. If everyone in the world today, living his or her present life, only realized that truth, this would be a much better place, wouldn't it?

CHAPTER 13

KARMA LINKS

Ingrid says that in every lifetime, we encounter people we have known in previous lives. Parents, siblings, friends and colleagues, lovers, partners, husbands and wives, children, in-laws, are all somewhat connected from the past. These would not have a memorable impact on us if there had been no previous connection to them. Families are encounters by divine appointment to challenge and advance each other in various realms of life. Adversaries are often rivals or enemies from the past.

Also connected are meaningful encounters with teachers, therapists, doctors, spiritual leaders who have a positive influence upon our life. Sometimes these connections can have a negative influence by manipulative and harmful behaviors. A missed diagnosis can be harmful to one's health and well being. In any case, those we seek out for guidance and help are often karmic ties from earlier lives. Netherton once said that we get the therapist we deserve.

Perhaps you had a violent father. This indicates you had violence in a past life. It will remain with you and perpetuate itself until you resolve it.

Or perhaps you had a problem with a possessive mother, as Gertrude did.

"Gertrude was 65 when she came to me. She told me she had always been dominated by the older woman. Although this person was now dead, Gertrude couldn't stop revolving her life around the maternal issue."

"My mother would never let me have any fun, she interfered with my marriage and she didn't like the way I raised my children," a despondent Gertrude told Ingrid at their first session.

"Was she like this with everyone?" Ingrid asked her.

"Not with my sister," was the bitter reply. "Ilsa got everything she wanted from her. If she planned to go out, she'd say 'Bye, Mama,' and our mother never said a word. But if I wanted to go somewhere, she'd throw a fit! When I was little, she would spank me because she said I was rebelling against her."

Gertrude looked rather defiant when she said this, adding "Well, of course I was. I couldn't let her get away with always telling me what to do!"

Ingrid gathered from their conversation that her client had been very aggressive and stubborn in dealing with her mother who, in turn, had been three times as dominant to her daughter as she might have been. This was a classic case of cause and effect in a dominating relationship: if you push, the other person will push even harder.

Now began a series of regressions. Finally, they broke through the woman's present life stresses. The troubling incident took place in a past life of a century or more ago, when our world was governed by patriarchy. Papas ruled the roost, for better or worse.

"I see my father, but he is like mama," Gertrude said in wonder.

"He's so cruel. He's made me marry a man I don't love. Papa is so cold and logical, and I hate him for it."

Now Ingrid had part of the puzzle. Gertrude was rebelling against this past father who in this life was now her mother. But there was more to her troubles than this past life, since we, as victims, repay past karmic debts for being a victimizer. So now Ingrid and her client hunted even further back in those past lives to find the time when Gertrude was the victimizer. And one day, in a life lived centuries ago, they found it.

Gertrude saw herself as a Roman Centurion, stationed in a desert community. In this life she was an arrogant man dressed in ancient armor and carrying a shield who was training other men. Oh, I'm so domineering," she said. "Women are like possessions to me! I take them as I please. I am a person who has no consideration for others or for their feelings."

One of those women she mistreated would later become her mother in this life. As the Centurion, she had died fairly young in battle.

They had now found all the pieces of the puzzle.

"I can't believe it," Gertrude marveled, as she realized what lay at the root of her lifelong obsession with her mother.

Now, finally, she could accept the fact that she was a very powerful person in her own right, something that she had repressed all her life. She had fought with her mother because of her own lust for power which she was projecting onto the other woman.

Ingrid points out that no matter what your age is, and Gertrude was 65, it is a relief to realize what you have been subconsciously doing to yourself. If someone tries to suppress you, it's over power not being used appropriately by you.

You can only be abused or kept in bondage if you, yourself, allow it. You have to subconsciously want the abuse. It's like a mirror. Other people can only treat you the way you treat yourself. Otherwise, you would get out. Others push in when you don't push out.

"Another of my clients, whom I will call Meg had a very good relationship in her past lives that continue to this day," Ingrid says.

Meg's regressions included a life in which she studied religion and then law before dying of ulcerative colitis. She had a brother of whom she was fond in that life, so in their next lifetimes, when he was now a woman, Meg chose him to be her mother. Theirs had been a good relationship in their earlier life together, and they would continue it in this one.

Friendships and good kinships often continue and build lifetime after lifetime. There is a basic law regarding relationships. We always resume an affiliation with other souls at the point we last left each other. If you lost someone you loved in a past life due to an early death, you may experience feelings of fear of loss when you meet that person again in this life.

If you two were rivals or enemies in that past life, you will experience a feeling of antipathy towards that person when you first meet them in today's world. And, if you betrayed or abandoned that other soul, you will feel guilty and perhaps even feel a compulsion to please them now.

This is why it's not a good idea to leave unresolved any conflicts between you and others in this life, or you will both have to pick up that connection at the same spot in your next one.

There is no end, for we will meet again in some future time until all imperfections are balanced out and transformed.

CHAPTER 14

PRENATAL AND BIRTH EXPERIENCES

Ingrid explains that the basis of all past life work is to start at the prenatal and birth experience. Everything that happens in pregnancy, even the music the mother plays, is picked up and stored by the baby growing within her body.

The baby that almost dies at birth but is saved by a doctor's wisdom remembers that "miracle." When grown, that person will run to a doctor for anything, because of the belief that "doctors can save me."

Ingrid's studies indicate that we pick our parents and the lives we lead in order to learn certain lessons in this life. The soul's hunger for life is so strong that it will even push a couple together in order to be born even in unfortunate circumstances. The hunger for life is as strong as the hunger for food.

The first time the mother realizes she is pregnant is the first greeting given her baby, and that baby will take it in and store it in its subconscious. If its impregnation is a disappointment, the baby will feel unwanted. In later years, he might go around expecting rejection and saying "I hope I'm not disturbing you."

If the mother is first happy about her pregnancy only to later reject it, the baby will grow up with the idea that relationships that start well will be followed by rejection. If she rejects her pregnancy only to accept it later, it could be fatal for her baby. The idea would be implanted that you can only be accepted through rejection.

Even the discussion of abortion is a very sensitive issue for the unborn as it is a threat to its life, explains Ingrid. The soul consciousness wanders in and out of the mother's body during gestation, but it experiences every trauma suffered by its mother, including that of birth. If there should be trouble in the home, accompanied by yelling and slapping of the mother, her fetus will also feel threatened.

When the birth process begins, the new baby reacts according to its character. Some can't wait to get out, while others want to return to the womb. The eager ones will easily tackle and welcome new situations in life while the others would like to put things off as long as possible.

Going through the birth canal is often traumatic. The birth cord no longer feeds the baby, and when the mother's water breaks there is a loss of protection. From the traumatic journey through the birth canal often comes fear of suffocation, a sense of pressure or not making it on time by the newborn.

The way we react to this trauma establishes how we handle stress in our later life.

Those of us who are delivered by Caesarian birth are deprived of our first battle for survival. Lacking this need to fight our way through, we could easily expect others to do our future battles for us. Or, oppositely, we may prefer to be very independent and to do everything ourselves because we didn't have to win our first success in this life.

Our birth struggle establishes our cycle of activity. Some of us who started birth easily only to face troubles at the end, such as a forceps delivery, may start fast but never finish projects in this life, those born quickly and easily may rush through to the ending of them, and those born prematurely may always appear impatient and trying to attempt tasks before they are ready.

It seems our karma is linked with that of our parents and that on some soul level we recognize each other.

In case of an impregnation from rape, the soul that becomes incarnate from this rape may have been too passive in a past life, but we've all lived too many lives to be only violent or passive personalities.

"I have discovered that when I find a person has had a violent personality in one lifetime, the next is usually full of fears which attract violence to them. Unfortunately, they are often afraid to fight for what they believe in," says Ingrid.

"I always recommend at least two to three life regressions on one topic to discover patterns that exist."

She explains that "Our souls pick the conception and even the genes they will inherit, the illnesses and the personality traits. Despite the scientific believe that the genetic and hereditary influences are paramount in our lives, conception also is tied in direct relationship with our karmic mission, which is to become a better person and to develop certain desirable traits. It takes the soul's awareness to activate the genes that are in alignment with the soul's task.

"After death our soul makes an accounting of its recent life, to bring those experiences to a conclusion. We come out of each lifetime asking such questions as "what have I achieved and developed?" Then we formulate a decision for our next karmic mission.

"What our soul in that time between lives decides it wants to do in the future isn't the same as actually doing it once we return in that new body."

According to Ingrid's findings, the life's review becomes very clear to the soul in the afterlife, but impeding factors may come in the way of our mission. They could be such things as letting our opportunities slip by or becoming overly success oriented once reincarnated in a new identity.

We incarnate into families that reflect our earlier lives. Our conception seldom comes at a boring, harmonious time but rather when a decision has to be made, for our soul is born with a desire to overcome odds and to achieve something in this present life. It loves conflict because this helps it evolve.

As Ingrid puts it, "Our beginnings and our ends are always related. From death evolves life and from life evolves death. Our personality is like a tree in that our trunk is made up of all our past lives, and its branches in this life are fed by those times and emotions.

"We continue to get emotional about similar issues, life after life. In each, though, the one basic necessity to solve is our karmic task. If our life ends well and we have progressed on our spiritual path, there will be no major distresses in our subsequent ones. If, however, we have caused suffering and death to others, we, in turn will suffer for it."

Ingrid has learned over the years that whatever comes up in a regression reflects a predicament that continues to be unresolved by that soul to this day. The important regressions are the dramatic ones, where death did not come easily and where the soul did not slip peacefully into that time between lives. Truly, the way of death often is the mirror to the way that person lived during that lifetime here on Earth.

The Asian saying: "you must first know how to die before you know how to live" reflects this. Only when our life is in order, we have made use of our possibilities and our relationships are in harmony, will death be a peaceful experience.

Our birth is the curtain between our lives, and it establishes our cycle of activity. Some of us will start fast, but never finish anything, while others will rush a project through to the ending.

Going through the birth canal is a traumatic time for us, for the uterus cord no longer feeds us. During our fight through the small vaginal opening, we have a fear of suffocation which can affect us all our life as claustrophobia. Our birth, in which we face the danger of death and suffocation, establishes the way we handle stress in this life. If we were pulled out by forceps, we may wait till the last minute to do anything as we get older.

Babies born by Caesarian operations are deprived of winning that first battle for life. This lack of fighting the way through to birth may cause some to always expect others to do for them. It may, conversely, cause them to want to be fiercely independent, to do everything for themselves.

Preemies, those who are born prematurely, are often impatient and want to do things before they're ready. Here's an interesting exercise for you:

1. Reflect on how you feel just before you meet new people. Are you excited? Curious? Apprehensive? That is a reflection of that first greeting you received in the womb.
2. Check the month you were conceived. That month is often the time you start new activities. Do you seem to be more active that month every year? Do you meet interesting new people?
3. Are there any months that you feel especially lively or passive or withdrawn? Healthy or weak? There are success oriented months and problem oriented ones.
4. How do you feel a few weeks before your birthday? Many mimic their mothers who were waiting to give you birth by feeling loggy. Several weeks after your birthday, you have renewed energy.
5. Try imagining your own birth. Who was there? Who brought your mother to the hospital? How did your mother feel about having you? Were there any stresses?
6. How do you feel on your birthday? Do you like to celebrate or is it a calm or solemn day?

The way we feel on our birthday is a reflection of how we felt right after our birth. Babies who were extremely exhausted usually don't like to celebrate their birthdays while the ones who were alert love to celebrate them. Hate your birthday? Wait and celebrate it in a couple of weeks later. You'll like it better.

CHAPTER 15

WHAT ABOUT TWINS?

In conducting past life regressions, says Ingrid Vallieres, "we first investigate our present lives and then our prenatal experiences. It is amazing what knowledge is acquired during those months we are in our mothers' wombs."

And what if you are sharing that womb with others, as in the case of twins and multiple births? Twins may be halves of a single egg physically, but their souls are separate entities.

Usually, they have shared previous lives. Their souls direct the mother's impregnation and, as with all embryos, they feel body consciousness from the beginning, although their real individual entities come at birth. Ingrid's example of such a case deals with Kristine and Sylvia.

The twins were 35 when Kristine came to her for a regression. Sylvia elected to go elsewhere for a similar one at the same time. Strangely, neither was aware the other was being regressed until much later. Essentially, both remembered the same instances of their births.

"Kristine had always been told that she was the older - and the healthier – twin," says Ingrid." Au contraire! We discovered during her regression that she was actually the younger of the two girls."

"I hear the midwife saying that Oh God, there's another coming," remembered Kristine. "I hear them talking about me, that I'm blue and that I need medical attention. Then the doctor tells the midwife, 'This baby won't make it much longer,' and they're talking about ME!"

Later in the session, it was learned that inadvertently the twin girls were mixed up, and the family thought Sylvia was the weak child. They pampered this child, fearing she would die. In fact, they even held an emergency baptism at the hospital for her because of this misapprehension.

Thus, the child who was born ill became the "well child" and the other, who was born healthy, became "the invalid." Kristine always felt the spoiling of her twin to be an "injustice," and it caused a great deal of tension and jealously between them.

After this prenatal regression, Kristine excitedly called Sylvia and told her what she had learned. To her surprise, Sylvia's recollections of their births dovetailed exactly with hers.

"I always thought something was wrong with the idea that Sylvia was so weak, and she did take advantage of it occasionally," Kristine told Ingrid at their next session.

At this one, they began exploring her past lives. As Ingrid suspected, Kristine and Sylvia had been rivals in several of their previous times on Earth.

"You see," says Ingrid, "all patterns of our lives are showing up in the prenatal period and are links to our past lives. Birth and death are the curtains between our lives, and our births always bring on some past life issues. We don't get a totally fresh start each lifetime. Souls pick up where it left off the last time they were together."

Another client, Cecily also realized she wasn't alone in her mother's womb.

As Ingrid explains it, "If you are a twin, a regression into your prenatal state reveals how in about .your third month in the womb you realize you aren't alone."

Cecily explained in her regression how she realized "there is something hard in here like me. It's irritating and amusing me. I'm curious about it. We smile at each other. But there isn't enough room. We're squashed, but it's nice and cozy. We try to share the room."

When the water bag burst during the birth, Cecily said she felt a pain. "My head is bursting. I'm suffocating, coughing, thrashing about."

The twin girls were born prematurely. They were so small and weak that an emergency baptism was performed on them for fear they would die.

In this case history, it is clear that since the first reaction between the girls was friendly in the womb it indicates they had a happy relationship in the past.

The experiences of other twins in the womb haven't always been as positive as in Cecily's case. Often souls who were past enemies meet again as twins. Take Helmut and his twin, for example.

When Helmut realized he was sharing the womb with another, he was angry. In his regression he recalled "For goodness sake, not again. I feel disturbed. When we get bigger, there is tension. I push him to the wall. I do not take any notice of him. My brother is just a shadow. I am entirely self centered."

Helmut also experienced his own fertilization.

"Funnel shaped threads are running together. I see an egg cell and seeds melting into one another. I am concentrating all my attention on it. I am enveloped in something grey-white. It's pleasant..."

Helmut's parents disagreed about this pregnancy. The mother had aborted an earlier fetus and was determined to carry this pregnancy to term. The father questioned if the babies were his.

Helmut experienced a great deal of fear during his birth because he had a hard time getting through the birth canal. After birth, he felt lonely and forsaken by his mother.

He said "nobody loves me. I'm sad, as though I know a lot of hardship is coming to me in life. I hate my brother. Pay attention to me! I'm the oldest! But they like him better. I have to take notice of him now."

Helmut had a big stress in his life about being recognized and loved by those around him.

His parents would hold his twin up to him as an example, and the relationship between the two men grew increasingly tense until his twin died at an early age of cancer. During his regressions, they learned that the two had caused a great deal of harm to each other in past lives.

You may wonder why two souls who were enemies would incarnate into such a close relationship. People and troubles we shoved away in the past will return with a vengeance in this life! The solution is that we have to accept and integrate what is bothering us, to bring us peace. Challenges are always given to us to help us grow spiritually.

CHAPTER 16

UNCOUNTABLE LIFETIMES

Past life work has reached a breakthrough in the past thirty years. Many of Ingrid's early clients were in awe when they discovered their past lives. Most were very much in doubt at first.

Today, her clients hardly ever doubt the existence of past lives, jumping right into regression. Past life work has become quite common, and regressions are accessible to everyone in therapy-oriented countries.

In many earlier eras, revelation of past lives was a privilege reserved for the initiation ceremonies. All knowledge of the mind, of healing, herbs, massage techniques that were used in earlier times by certain cultures are experiencing a renaissance.

The Aquarian Age is the therapeutic age, the era of broadening the awareness of the soul as well as the era of technology. Thus, all previous forms of therapies are now revived. We never had so many therapies coexisting as we do now.

"During my years of study, many of my questions about life were answered when I studied the influence of past lives to our current existences," says Ingrid." I learned why we react to people in a certain way, what karmic connections led us to incarnate in certain families, and why we get involved with certain people. Whatever our mutual history was before determines what kind of relationship we will have with that person in this life. We are building on the groundwork laid out in earlier lives."

Early on, after her near death experience in Japan, Ingrid became as enthusiastic as her friend Roland was in these studies, because she finally found a logical explanation to many stresses people face that are not just explained by a difficult childhood.

"In my own case, I would have never enrolled in psychotherapy, because I didn't consider myself stricken with complications. I was, however, very curious to find out about my past and to uncover those layers of memory that I felt I had. As I did this regression work to find my true self, I also solved my own problems. Automatically, when you work with your past, the subconscious will offer up unresolved issues."

During one of Ingrid's early sessions dealing with her own life, she resolved one fear she had since childhood, a deadly fear of spiders.

She remembers saying once to a girlfriend, "Can you imagine how terrible it would be if spiders could fly?"

"We had a garden, and spiders occasionally crawled into our house through windows and doors. I was so sensitive to the crawling things that I would wake up at night, if a spider were anywhere in my room. The thought of spiders flying onto me was my recurring nightmare," she says.

Although this was obviously a problematic behavior, she would not have considered therapy for it. She learned, however, that whatever is created by our imagination is a re-creation of a past event which we have experienced but not successfully mastered.

"In one of my regressions," she says, "I saw myself in a desert-like stony landscape. There was a tree. Hiding in that tree, was a huge spider which ultimately dropped down and crushed me to death. This related exactly to my nightmare of spiders - huge and "flying.""

After she worked through that regression, she discovered that her fear of spiders was gone, and she didn't encounter another spider in that environment.

"There is a magnetic attraction between the person who has a fear and the cause of that fear. What you reject and dislike, you attract."

Much later this development evolved into another stage of being confronted again with spiders until Ingrid finally could see them as friendly and quite stunning animals.

"All organisms try to survive by eating each other, so there is no reason to sulk if, during a few of our lives, we just fall victim to the food chain!"

In regression work, fears are handled by directly addressing them and questioning their survival issue. When looking at a difficult subject, for example an illness, a fear will be part of that problem and thus handled.

Perhaps you suffer from headaches. During a regression, you might find you were beheaded in a marketplace in the Middle Ages where there were many people present watching and scorning you. Not just the headache might be explained but also a possible fear of people and a fear of rejection.

Another of Ingrid's own early childhood distresses was travel sickness. She would become sick whether in a car, a bus, an airplane or on a boat at sea. She began to look at this enigma during her various regressions. Where in the world did this come from, she wondered.

She had to work through several lifetimes to solve that one.

"I learned that in one lifetime, I was incarcerated and then put on a cart with a linen sack over my head and taken to my death. In another life, I died of exhaustion after a tiresome journey, and another time I died at sea when my ship went down. That time, I was a prisoner, stowed in a lower deck. To my subconscious, travel meant involuntarily being abducted and forced to go on a deadly journey."

As much as Ingrid loves to travel in this life, the difference between the present and her former lives is that she can choose her destination and travel on her own volition rather being forced.

She explains that there is a distinct difference between symptoms and difficulties. A headache is a symptom, but the stress stems from an inner conflict that hasn't been resolved. Many therapies just touch on the symptoms but, with the therapy of cause and effect, you take the symptom as a lead to the difficulty. One problem can cause many symptoms, which is why past life therapy is so effective because it gets back to the origin of your stresses. It isn't necessary to handle each and every symptom separately. When you get to the root of your trauma, which we call the core pattern, all symptoms are explained and can be handled.

For example, a fear of being rejected may bring about various manifold symptoms, such as feeling out of place, constantly trying to please, dissatisfaction with one's looks, being overly ambitious, over stressed and so on. Once the underlying issue is addressed, all is well.

Some of Ingrid's most frequently asked questions are "how many lifetimes do we have?" and "how far back does our history go?"

She explains that before there was a practical method to retrieve our past lives, many assumptions grew up. Rudolf Steiner's' anthroposophy school claims we have seven lifetimes as a male and seven as a female. Others say we have ten lifetimes all together. The Vedic scriptures say we have millions of lifetimes in the mineral, plant and animal kingdoms before we even become human and then have many more as humans.

Ingrid's findings indicate there is a gradual evolution from a pure soul consciousness into a material and physical consciousness which can take eons of time.

You and I have lived uncountable lifetimes. Not only have we lived thousands of lives as humans, but perhaps we were even there in the early earth evolution of mineral, plant and animal life consciousness.

Our body is composed of billions of cells that have their genetic memories in the far past of the earth as well as in space.

Scientists know that the atoms that make up our body have partially originated from outer space. This corresponds exactly to the evolution of the soul. In its original state, there is pure soul consciousness. It then separates to turn to individual consciousness which implies polarity and duality, time and distance, and energy that gradually densifies into matter. Thus, soul manifests on the mental, energy and material plane. The soul's individual development may very well correspond to the evolution of the universe. It may well be that the soul has lived on many planets.

CHAPTER 17

MANY APPROACHES TO REGRESSION

Over the years, Ingrid has continued to restructure the therapy techniques she learned from different sources. She works on distinguishing symptoms from problems, for symptoms can be a red herring to distract from the real underlying stresses.

Ingrid notes there are a number of approaches to past life work - psychic readings, symbolic, problem oriented, non problem oriented, hypnotic and non hypnotic.

PSYCHIC READINGS - You go to a psychic who "reads you" by tapping into your energy field or subconscious. Sometimes the psychic can pick up on a true image that can be helpful, but the client usually misses any personal experiences with this method.

SYMBOLIC THERAPY - With this, therapists use subliminal images to access the subconscious. For example, as your therapist Ingrid might ask you to imagine you are going down many floors in an elevator. The lower it goes, the more you can tap into your subconscious. Or she might ask you to imagine diving into the ocean for a pearl or seeing an old man sitting in a cave, holding a book that contains all the information about your past. These might be images, flashbacks and even stories that may surface containing useful information.

There is no guarantee, however, that this approach will bring up any strong issues you need to get resolved. Usually in this approach, the therapist only accompanies the patients and encourages them to go further back in time. They only look at the image. No probing questions are asked to lead you into a functional experience of this past life. Usually, this type of approach is a preparation for the problem-oriented therapy, and it can also be used well on children.

PROBLEM-ORIENTED - In this method, the focus is on emotions, fears, pains, failures and difficult relationships or career-related problems. One issue is defined and the patient is regressed to the specific lifetime where this incident emerged, implying handling of past issues, traumas and guilt or failure.

NON-PROBLEM ORIENTED - With this, the patient is told to count back 50 or 100 years. Either the hypnosis or relaxation technique is used to get them there. Sometimes the therapist might focus on positive issues, with questions such as "which countries did you like or "what kind of lifetime are you experiencing."

This would include symbolic therapy, interesting pictures as well as real stories which may arise containing clues to better understand your present life.

The patient faces no deep seated problems with this method, and there is little or no therapeutic effect. What emerges in such regressions can be insignificant or boring. Sometimes there comes out what we call the "Caesar/Cleopatra" wishful thinking in which they fantasize that they were an historical figure in a previous lifetime. This may or may not be a true, relevant picture.

HYPNOTIC - In this approach, hypnosis is used to block out the analytical mind and to access the subconscious without the mind interfering.

The advantage of this method is the quicker access to the subconscious. The disadvantage is that the client can be manipulated by the therapist's questions.

Under this method, the client can only experience that former life as it was but cannot understand it on an analytical basis nor integrate it into the present time. At the end of the session, the analytical mind must confront what has been uncovered. This can be very traumatic to afterwards identify with and confront what has been uncovered.

Many therapists use hypnosis to bring their clients into their past lives. Some clients resist hypnosis in the fear that they might be manipulated. Ingrid notes that hypnosis has many levels, and sometimes a relaxation technique is also called hypnotic induction.

Since our subconscious is already overloaded with hypnotic experiences in past lives, such as manipulation, suggestions, rituals, brainwashing, Ingrid personally would rather refrain from using hypnotic induction. The regression work is geared toward unburdening the subconscious from past influences and not to put new suggestions on top of the old. Even our conclusions and decisions we took at the time of death in past lives act as self-hypnosis.

NON-HYPNOTIC - This is the one Ingrid uses. She will ask the client to tell her the first image that comes into their mind. Before entering into the regression, a past life image is being created by associative questions, for example, "What feelings are connected with this image?" or "What would be the worst situation causing you a certain feeling?"

The spontaneous technique used at the beginning of the regression prevents the analytical mind from interfering.

Ingrid will say, "Your subconscious is going to present us now with the past life incident that will resolve this issue. Tell me the first image that comes to mind. What do you see?"

The client gradually slips into the incident and becomes more and more absorbed by the unfolding event. At this stage, present time is totally forgotten and you will become completely identified with the past.

Much attention is given to undoing all unwanted connections and knots tying the present to the past. This requires a good grasp of the workings of the mind and can only be performed by a trained therapist.

Regression itself reveals the past incident, but it will not provide the necessary links to tie the past with the present. This comparison is done after the regression has been completed as to enable the analytical mind to understand the current behavior as it has been formed or influenced by your past.

To relieve the present from the past is the utmost goal of past life regression.

The voice of the therapist provides a tool to help the client to access his or her past lives.

When Ingrid induces a regression, she keeps her voice deep and slow, thus guiding the subconscious into locating an incident. To bring someone out of regression, she speaks faster and in a higher voice.

Any state in the client can be manipulated by talking slowly and in a deeper voice. To calm others down, she speaks slowly and in short sentences to allow the client's subconscious to locate what it's looking for. To snap the subject out of this self-induced trance, the secret is to speak faster and higher, making long sentences.

"People often ask why I don't use hypnosis in my therapy sessions. They wonder how you can otherwise access the subconscious mind. There are several reasons. The therapist can, without intending to do so, tamper with your memory. Commands may be harmful in this type of induction because they may trigger past life commands and awaken an earlier hypnotic incident which may mix up the incidents trying to be accessed.

"Also, when the client is in a trance, he or she is out of present time and cannot reject commands or questions that should be rejected. In a hypnotic state, one can't always block any type of suggestions made but will be inclined to take any question asked as a suggestion, which will be followed, for the client won't hear it as a question. They are that identity and will tend to accept any type of command given. For all these reasons, many people are just naturally resistant to hypnosis and will not allow anyone to put them under," Ingrid says.

"In a non hypnotic state, both one's awareness levels, the analytic and subconscious, work together. That's why one can relive the experience while looking at it objectively. In the hypnosis approach, since the client isn't linked to the present time, he or she can only become and respond as this other personality they have entered. One might talk like a child, or the personality now uncovered may have been retarded or even deaf, so the client can't hear the questions asked during the session."

Whatever method is applied, the key to a successful therapeutic work is the trust between the therapist and the client. The ethical code of any therapist using his or her skills should lie in the best interest of the client. Respect, responsibility and careful consideration in handling every case are the basis of a professional entrusted with the health, faculty and well being of the patient.

The regression leads the client carefully to view all the aspects and situations of that former life, reliving emotions, voicing thoughts, dialogues and resolutions, describing his or her own role in that life as well as the important people which could be regarded as "players" or comrades in that earlier setting. Childhood, adulthood and major decisions and events, changes of course of action, troubles, hardships, happy moments – all these offer a complete biography that has evolved at the end of the session.

"After the regression, the most important task lies ahead," says Ingrid. "Now we must integrate the incident and understand its effect on your present life. If this integration isn't brought to a successful conclusion, your regression will not contribute to your evolution or your understanding of what happened so long ago.

"In my work, I use no input not originated by the client. Nor do I alter one word of what he or she says. I record the exact words expressed, and I never evaluate what is said or alter it into another statement. If one word is altered, the client's subconscious will go into another channel.

"I never add to the client's story, because the ego always looks for an excuse to avoid looking at its problems. If the therapist adds to the story or makes personal suggestions, the client will reject the story afterwards. In this approach, the original data the client offers is used to uncover the hidden past life incident. I do not add or subtract, but I just build on the data voiced by the client.

"It's also necessary to insist that my questions be answered in spite of the client's hesitation or discomfort. Unanswered questions leave a void and a sense of dissatisfaction.

During the traumatic part of the incident, I ask the client to feel the pain and the emotion, and feel his or her body. Re-experiencing the physical aspect of the trauma will release it." Ingrid is always careful not to be pulled into a regression until she knows the client.

Some may be psychotic. When faced with a new client who turns out to have mental problems, it's vital to be able to control the situation. This is why voice training is very important for a past life therapist. If, for example, a person shows psychotic signs while in a past life regression, it is vital to keep him or her in touch with the incident and move the client through it to the end. As soon as the pain and trauma are released, signs of psychotic behavior usually will cease.

In past life work, a psychosis is defined as being stuck in an old death trauma and compensating it by indulging in manias, hysterics or other wild behaviors. Trauma in this case means a threat to life, physical and mental pain, injury, abuse or a painful or sudden death. To relieve trauma is the target for regression therapy.

Past guilt can also trigger psychotic behavior in this life, because it's a way of evading the former misdeed and at the same time imposing a disorder on oneself.

Both the voice and control of the therapist can handle even difficult or extreme situations arising in therapy. With psychotic people, or those who tend to lose control, it's vital for the therapist to use authority in speaking and to express a strong presence. The subconscious will always go along with a therapist who demonstrates a healthy control over the session.

"When we delve into past lives, we never know what will happen," says Ingrid. "This is the unknown factor. Every life has many layers of secrecy and repression; therefore the therapist must be prepared for anything, including the appearance of strong emotions, physical reactions and over reactions. I always advise my therapist trainees to be careful to start practicing regressions only after they're properly trained, then they have the self confidence, know-how and experience they need to successfully lead the client through any type of regression."

CHAPTER 18

SELF INDUCING YOUR OWN REGRESSION

People often ask Ingrid if and how they can regress themselves. There are a number of people willing to help you do this by means of tapes or write-ups, although not all are therapists who are properly trained. But, as she learned in her earlier experiences with regression techniques, you will be able only to get pictures ("snapshots") of those lives. Without a trained therapist to guide you, it is not possible to get the full deeper subconscious insights from true regressions.

"I do not encourage self-imposed regressions with tapes, incense or other things," she says. "With a curious, open mind and a desire to find out what happened in your past, you may tap into such images. Unfortunately, if this is tried when alone, you may fall into an unsettling situation or perhaps even uncover a piece of a trauma from the past. A person can't guide himself through a past life. It can't be relived and at the same time you can't answer the necessary questions that might arise. The purpose of regression therapy is to be able to relive and learn from one's past lives."

Ingrid points out that many people get occasional flashbacks of previous lives. A child may visit an American Civil War battlefield and remember dying in the battle that took place there. Another may visit an ancient house where they remember and even find a hidden doorway to a secret room.

These memories of a past life are like glimpses or a quick flash of a previous life.

Children access their past very easily, because they don't try to alter reality as much as adults do who often only want to be right and who have fixed opinions on life.

"We can induce our own past life explorations, although it would be difficult for us to perform any necessary therapy on ourselves. After all, how many doctors operate on their own appendixes?" asks Ingrid.

Those wishing to explore their past on their own can find a number of regression tapes on the market today. You can even tape your own. These are based on self hypnosis which offers certain suggestions to help one access their subconscious memories. Some suggest the use of candlelight, incense, crystals or the sound of a metronome.

There are a number of ways to uncover one's own past life characteristics.

Let's take locations, for an example. Which cities, regions and countries do you like? Are there places you like to travel to where you feel comfortable and at home? Are there places you have never been but long to visit?

What kinds of feelings arise when you think about them or go there? What kind of experience could you have had in these places? Use your imagination to get pictures, costumes, the faces of people, their lifestyle. What was your role? How was your everyday life? What were the important features of that lifetime?

If you enjoy mountains, you may have lived a lifetime in them. The life may have been peaceful or upsetting, but something still wants to be relived and possibly taken to a good ending. On the other hand, if you feel very uncomfortable in a certain city or country, you may have had a serious political problem or an accident leading to your death.

Our close family ties which include our relatives, spouses, children, friends and enemies are usually people we have known before. How does that person seem to you? What roles do you play with each other?

Ask yourself what your relationship might have been such as parent or child, sibling, superior or inferior, judge or convict? Again, your feeling reveals what happened in the past.

How would this relationship have ended? What were the good things or the disappointing events about your former relationship? Why are you together again? What is the learning task, what should be accomplished between the two of you so that you don't leave a traumatic happening unsolved that will only show up again in a later life? What is the potential of your relationship? Which traits and strengths can best be developed from it?

Only when you learn to accept the other person's personality while understanding your own feelings and reactions will you be able to learn the lesson of why you had to meet again. Perhaps it's to overcome mistakes and omissions of your part and to accept that different people pursue different goals. Despite clashes, the basic personality is good and needs to be accepted and recognized.

What are your hobbies? Which activities do and did you enjoy most in school or as a pastime? What are your talents? What traits still need to be developed? For example, while tennis or golf can be a hobby today, possibly in an earlier life you dealt with precision engineering or building combat tools such as cannons that shot balls into another territory. Your life and prestige depended on the successful working of the tools.

Then there are your emotions. What are your main emotions during the day or during happy and unhappy times? What is your basic emotion? Are some of these blocked? Do you deny yourself certain emotions? Do positive ones last or do they die quickly? What was your most intense emotion in this life and what caused it? What would be the worst situation in a past life that would cause you to have this emotion? What would be the event most desired in your life that would make you totally happy? When could a similar event have happened in an earlier life?

Pleasant or unpleasant emotions both stem from traumas. If you feel happy or exhilarated when you have won a game or have passed an exam, you may have won a game in the past that overcame a threat to your life. In our past lives, losers were often put to death, such as were the gladiators or in man to man combat. Fear, anger, sadness, depression and such feelings are always directly linked to a situation causing death. On the other hand, victors were sometimes put to death as in the winner of the Mayan ball games. He would be sacrificed to the gods. In such a case, winning a game today after such a past life death from victory, the soul might decide losing is preferable. Beautiful women in the past were sometimes chosen as involuntary sacrifices, raped or made into temple prostitutes. That soul today might hide by deliberately making herself unattractive.

Regressions uncover such incidents as wars and the violence, aggression and losses sustained from them; suppression by greedy kings, emperors or dictators where the problems evolve around the fight for survival, hunger, threat, losses, injustice and hatred.

The effects of such earlier lifetimes show up in exhaustion and stress symptoms such as depression or fear of loss. Effects of these can include unrealistic expectations, fear of using one's own strength and even snobbery or feeling you are better than others.

Everyone has also played authoritarian roles in which they ruled over others, whether in a family clan, a tribe, as landowner, leading an expedition or an army. Perhaps you were a government official or held a high ranking position such as an aristocrat or religious leader. You might have been anything from the patriarch or matriarch of a family to a king or queen, high priest or priestess or even a pope.

Since power is often abused for egotistical purposes, these roles may foster injustices, cruelties, impose unnecessary hardship on so-called inferiors, be greedy or vain, ultimately causing the downfall of that group or organism. The effect of previous power abuse may today manifest itself as low self esteem and being afraid of using one's potentials and talents in this life. Often formerly authority figures attract injustice and are wrongfully accused of various wrongdoings. The soul often bounces from one extreme to another in the attempt to balance its life.

In another regression, you might remember a life as a priest or magician, for religious roles covers some grounds in our past. They contain the quest for solving the mystery of life, and include self denial, ascetics, hypocrisy, illusion and delusion. If power were exerted over others it might have been through hypnosis and seduction. Good potentials and wisdom may have been jeopardized and lost due to vanity, lies and treachery for the sake of material and worldly aims. Sexuality is often abused by religious figures as a means to dominate and to manipulate.

Some of the roles in such a life could also have been as yogi, hermit, herb woman, sorcerer or sorceress, preacher, priestess, monk, nun, shaman, medicine man, black magician or hypnotist.

The effect of such lifetimes can cause one to be easy to influence, being gullible, naive, too trusting of religious cults, philosophies or political leaders and their parties.

Another lifetime could have been lived as a Casanova or bon vivant where you enjoyed a lifetime of amusements, playing with relationships, laughing off all commitments and denying responsibility. The troubles in such a life often arises when others are betrayed or true love is rejected. Then the light heartedness turns to sorrow and regret. As a consequence, the spirit condemns the amusing and joyful aspects of a future life.

In such a lifetime, you could have been a vagabond, gypsy, Don Juan, seducer, society lady, prostitute, mistress, concubine, musician or artist. Effects of such a lifetime could be a fear of closeness and disappointment in others as well as being very strict and self-disciplined.

Some lifetimes are cut short through natural catastrophes, such as floods, tidal springs, fires, lightning, earthquakes, storms, plagues, illnesses or starvation. Traumas arising from such catastrophes may cause you to have all kinds of fears for the future, for loss, be fearful of water, fire, heights and of sudden intervention. Since violence causes the body to hurt and to be mortally injured, you might also suffer asthma, respiratory problems, headaches, back pains, circulatory problems and other such ailments.

In some lives, we find ourselves in such professional roles as engineers, architects, scientists, smiths, construction workers, midwives, doctors, or astrologers, on whose knowledge the life of others depended. If our professional judgments were wrong, resulting in a lost life, we might have been accused and killed or suffered from guilt for the rest of our lives. Failure in an earlier life will bring about insecurity and fear of responsibility in this life.

Past lives are like archetypes and correspond to the basic colors of a prism. We have lived through all the basic experiences, says Ingrid, but the shades of the colors and their combinations make up our personality.

"Some of us have more attention on one area than on another, but in the end of a completed past life therapy all basic issues must be covered and a variety of all major types of past lives should have been regressed. Likes and dislikes lose their intensity, and life is taken at its best in this, our present time.

"In all our past lives, there are good and bad times, but sometimes the sad moments overshadow the happy ones. In therapy, while we are focusing on the issues faced by the client which often lead to traumatic memories, once the trauma has been experienced we can then bring forth the good times as well.

"All experiences are equal, and the freedom to choose any venue without karmic repercussions is restored. Now you can see why I believe we need professional help in uncovering our past lives. We need to understand our past, not just visit it."

CHAPTER 19

GINA WAS INTRIGUING

Gina is one of Ingrid's most intriguing clients.

Lies, deceptions, power quests, indifference to others and headstrong arrogance troubled Gina's life, although her initial complaint was her fear of exams and her rebellion against any kind of authority.

One of her many regressions took place during the Roman Empire, another in Medieval Europe and an even earlier regression took her to an ancient country which existed in what would become Greece, possibly around the time of the Dorian invasion in 12,000 B.C. Ingrid says "possibly" because in regressions, it's often hard to exactly pinpoint the era as seen through the eyes of the client.

Ingrid met Gina in 1995 while teaching a seminar on naturopathy. Her approach lay in helping the students learn about the psychological impact of illness. They did some illness analyses during this class.

A young woman phoned Ingrid late one afternoon a few weeks after the conclusion of this seminar.

"Hello, this is Gina," she said when Ingrid answered. "I met you during that speech you gave my class on naturopathy."

"Yes, of course," Ingrid said, quickly riffling through her memory of the students who had come up to talk after the seminar. She couldn't really place the voice.

"I need to talk with you. I - I think you can help me," she said, hesitatingly. "What did you want to talk to me about?" Ingrid asked.

"I - I don't know where to begin," Gina said, again with hesitation in her voice. After a little prodding, she said she had begun hating her life and herself.

"I've got to take an exam soon, and I'm terrified," she confided.

"Why?"

"I don't know. I've always been afraid of any kind of test, and I have another problem, too. It's authority. I hate anyone telling me what to do," she confided, "and another thing, I hate to make decisions about anything. I really do."

And, as Ingrid was to discover in a series of regressions she performed on Gina the client had a further problem. Her life seemed full of lies and deception: where was the truth?

Her conversation intrigued Ingrid who arranged for Gina to come in for a consultation.

Her secretary announced the newcomer's arrival. The young woman was twenty minutes early and, whispered the secretary, seemed agitated.

"Hmm, this woman definitely has some kind of difficulty," Ingrid thought and said she would see her immediately.

"I observed her as she entered my office. Now I remembered her from my seminar, although we had never spoken. She sat in the back row of the room that day, quietly taking notes.

"Gina was a petite, slim woman, around 30 years old. Her hair was dark and clipped short, and she wore no makeup or jewelry except for the plain gold wedding band on her finger. Her earthen colored clothes were simple. She appeared to be quiet and conservative in nature. But she was shredding her thin handkerchief into tiny ribbons as she sat before me."

Ingrid began her usual preliminary interview. Gina told her she was married, with two children, and that she held several jobs. Not only did she work as a clerk in an office, but she was also a naturopath who gave massages in her spare time.

"I feel I'm living a life of lies," she said.

Her biggest difficulty, she thought, lay with her family who had always treated her with indifference.

"My mother was a beautiful woman who never had time for me. There were always men around her, and I knew that some were her lovers. I've become just like her," Gina moaned.

"You've had many lovers?" Ingrid studied her reaction.

"No, of course not, but I've had one affair since I married my husband. You see? Like mother, like daughter," she said rather bitterly.

In their first regression, Ingrid proceeded to take her client through her childhood and back to her prenatal memories. They were a shocker. It seemed that Gina's birth father was actually her supposed father's brother Albert. Gina's mother lied to her husband when she discovered she was pregnant. Even Gina's older sister, Lisa was conceived by another man.

She also remembered during this regression that there was a boy whom her mother said was a nephew. It was really her son by another lover.

"Mother disappeared once for a very long time. She was visiting and supposedly nursing a sick sister. The sister pretended she had the baby and took over raising him, but he was always visiting us."

Ingrid asked her to remember her pre-birth experiences.

"Mother and Uncle Albert are making love, and I am already conceived. There's a noise.

Mother's yelling at Lisa, to get out. She'd come into the bedroom and found them together. Lisa's only three years old. She doesn't understand what they're doing," Gina said dreamily.

"My mother lies. She lies about everything and she lies to everyone. I suppose from now on I'll have to think of Uncle Albert as my father and my father as my educator," mused Gina.

It was the beginning of a number of sessions. During another regression sometime later, Ingrid took her back to another life to discover why she was so fearful of exams.

"What do you see?" she asked in a slow, deep voice.

Gina began talking in a hesitant voice at first. As she went further into the regression, she talked faster and more evenly about that past life.

"I'm in my house. It's so bare. Hardly any furniture. I'm wearing a long skirt that feels very rough and some kind of blouse or shirt. Now, I'm walking out of my home. I see a forest behind it. I'm looking back at my house. Oh, it's -it's just a hut. We're so poor," said Gina.

"Tell me what happened to you in this life."

"I have a husband, but he doesn't love me. He has a lover, and she hates me. She wants to marry my husband. No! They've told the authorities that I'm a witch. Liars!

"Now I'm in court. They're examining me, trying to get me to confess. No, no. I am no witch, don't you understand? But they've found me guilty as charged. I'm to be burned at the stake.

"The flames, oh, they hurt. My clothes and my hair are on fire. I'm dying," she said, tears streaming down her face.

"Why did your husband betray you with another woman?"

"Now I see why. It's because I was cold to him, and I took him for granted. I pushed him away. I pushed him to that other woman," she said in a calmer voice.

"That regression ended there. Now we knew where some of her fears of tests and examinations came from. But we knew there was still more to explore" says Ingrid.

In another regression, they decided to go deeper into this fear of exams and competition. This time, Gina saw herself as a man, a leader of a religious group of Christians sometime in the 1st or 2nd century A.D. As Ingrid says, it is difficult to set an exact date in most regressions, it seemed to have taken place when Rome ruled and taxed the countryside.

These early Christians followed the Ten Commandments to the letter; they believed all humans are equal; and they rebelled against the forced conscription of their labor by the state. They refused to pay taxes to Rome.

Gina described these people as wearing simple, earthen colored robes of coarse linen, tied with cords around the middle. Their costumes reminded her of pictures she'd seen of the early Essenes.

"We were practicing passive resistance, not open rebellion," Gina remembered.

"A man on horseback is riding into our village. He's telling us he's from the city, and that this is our last chance to pay the taxes we owe. But we will not. We say that no power in the world can influence us to go against our beliefs. I'm the spokesman for our group, and I tell the horseman proudly that we won't ever change our minds.

"We're rounded up by other soldiers a few days later and marched barefoot to the city. All of us are taken, including the women and children. We go before a judge who condemns us for blasphemy because we worship only our God and Jesus Christ, not Caesar. Our young people are condemned to forced labor. The rest of us will be put to death. I tell them that I wish they would crucify me as they did our Lord Jesus Christ, but they laugh at me. I am hung and my neck is broken. And as I lay dying, I think how all these deaths could have been prevented, if I hadn't refused to go along with Rome's wishes. I made the decision for everyone. It is I, only I who should have died. I, alone. I had no right to determine the fate of my friends."

And that explained Gina's unwillingness to take sides in any controversy. Instead, she preferred to listen to all sides before she made up her mind, and she found it hard to come to a decision.

Ingrid notes that there was a disturbing arrogance and persistent personality emerging from these sessions. It seemed this soul had an unrealized trauma in that it always seemed to pull things down to destruction and especially self destruction, through its unbending need for power. Where did this headstrong arrogance come from? Obviously, there was more to this story.

And so they came to the regression that would explain so much about her biggest dilemma.

As usual, Ingrid carefully led Gina back into a past life. This one was much farther back than they had ever before regressed.

"Where are you now?"

"I'm in a temple, the temple of a goddess. My parents have brought me here to serve her.

I'm very young, maybe eight years old.

"A young woman in white, she must be about twelve or thirteen, comes and takes me to a room. It's more like a cell. The window is so high up I can't even see out of it. No one ever talks to me.

One of the priestesses brings my food to me. I'm given only fruit and some water to drink. I get very sleepy every time I drink the water. It's drugged. It makes me see pretty lights everywhere, and I don't care about anything.

"They give me dance lessons with other girls who seem to be around my age. They like my dancing, because they keep watching me. I never get to meet any of the other dancers. I wonder who they are.

"Now, all the other dancers have left. I am being taught another dance, the dance of love.

It has lots of turns and serpentine movements.

"The priestess who is teaching me the dance tells me I have been chosen to do it for our goddess who is young and who loves to have young girls around her temple and worshiping her. But I am warned that my dance and our ceremonies must please our goddess in order to save our world.

"It was this priestess's duty, she tells me, to choose The Dancer. She explains that those who run the temple look for a girl who is talented and mature enough to someday perform the highest sacrifices of the temple. If the dance is performed correctly, the dancer will unite with the goddess.

"I learn that I will be the only dancer who will be allowed to enter and perform in the holy hall of the goddess. I'm so excited. To serve our goddess! What a great honor.

Ingrid instructed Gina now to go forward two years in time. She continued her story.

"I am now around ten years old. "I practice my dance of love for a long time until I do it well enough to please the goddess. At first, I don't like the flute and drums that make up the music. The sounds come from an adjoining room, I think. I'm made to drink bitter grape juice.

"On the day of my final initiation to become a priestess, I am bathed in water scented with the fragrance of some kind of flower. Then I am dressed in soft, white linen draperies, gold shoes and many jewels.

"I am ushered into the holy hall. The beautiful goddess stands there. She's covered with precious stones, and a gold serpent twines itself around her. More, larger jewels adorn her eyes, making them look as if they have rays of light, called the "light of love" shining from them in the brilliant sunlight that radiates through the wall openings. Around the goddess's feet are bowls of what seem to be diamonds and gold. One seems to contain animal blood.

"I realize later that our goddess is a marble statue, very big, but when I see her for the first time, it's as though she lives and breathes. I am awestruck at the sight, "But what is this? Another young girl, around 14 years old, is there, kneeling at the altar. Is she also a dancer? No, she is one of the priestesses who watched me in the dance classes. But I sense she is afraid. Why? The priestess, who has become my only friend as well as my trainer, stands in front of the girl. I gasp as I watch her lift her sword.

"'Dance,' she commands me. The music starts and I begin my dance of love. I keep dancing to the goddess as my trainer turns to speak to the girl.

"'Take the sword. You must do the act, because if I do it the goddess will be angry and you will be damned for all eternity. Remember, if the goddess doesn't accept your sacrifice, the curse will hit us all,' she says sternly, "She gives the sword to the girl who hesitates for a moment before plunging it into her body. As I dance and watch the sacrifice, I worry. Will our goddess like my dance?

"The priestess is now the high priestess with the death of this other girl. She picks up a silver bowl and catches the sacrificial blood spurting out of the dying priestess. Then she motions me to stop the dance and come over to her. She hands me the bowl and urges me to drink. I don't want to do it, but she says I must. Some day, I will be the high priestess, she tells me.

"'The goddess showed mercy on you and you will serve her now and show it by drinking her blood,' she adds.

"I am appalled at what has happened, and I'm confused. I don't know what I feel, but there is gladness that the goddess accepted my dance. I am also happy that I will move up to a higher rank in our temple. I'm afraid of the sacrifice I just saw, but I am joyful that we have saved the world from destruction. What a terrible responsibility is held by my temple! We are the only ones who stand between catastrophe and our world.

"As time passes, I am taught the great secrets and rituals of the temple. We fear not pleasing the goddess and bringing her wrath down upon all our people. We don't exactly know what kind of fury she will exhibit, if not pleased. Some say the earth, herself, will wither and die.

"The days, weeks and months go by. Once a month, a girl is sacrificed while I dance my dance of love. On the rare occasions that a girl refuses to die by her own hand, the high priestess performs the act for her."

Ingrid instructed Gina again to go forward in time in this life.

"Two more years have passed. Now the high priestess is telling me that the time of supreme sacrifice is at hand. She will sacrifice herself to the goddess, and it will be my turn to accept her present role. She seems so happy. She's barely fourteen years old, but she isn't afraid of what lies ahead.

"'Remember, it's for the higher good of the temple for the high priestess to sacrifice herself. It's a gift for all my work and I will live in the garden with the goddess forever,' she says as she smiles at me.

"I have already chosen and trained the new temple dancer, the girl who will replace me first as dancer and then, some day, as high priestess.

"Now, the day of sacrifice is at hand. The new girl dances her dance of love, while I watch the high priestess lift up the sword and, without any hesitation, thrust it into her stomach. As she lies dying, I gather her blood in the silver bowl. I give it to the dancer to drink. I, who once was the dancer and then the trainer, am now high priestess.

"Life goes on - the weekly sacrifices, the daily rituals, the worry as to whether or not the goddess will be pleased at our sacrifices and dances.

"Sometimes I have to perform the killing. One victim is so frightened at the idea. She is around eleven years old, and she cries as she refuses the sword. I remember the day she was brought to our temple unwillingly by several ugly looking men. After we took her to her room, she spent most of her time crying for her family. Now she is crying again.

"'Do not be afraid of death.' I tell her. 'Death is only the threshold to our eternal goddess. Think of it. Your life to be given for the life of the world! Do it of your own volition, so our goddess won't be angry.'

"But she still won't do it, so I must. It is my first sacrificial kill, and it's hard to push in the sword, as she screams and carries on.

"It is so silly of her, I think, to be sad at going to the realm of the goddess.

"Our goddess always seems to approve of our sacrifices, as nothing catastrophic ever occurs. I find, however, that I am very lonely, because we are never permitted to befriend each other in this temple. I have no friends here."

Again, Ingrid instructed Gina to go forward in time.

"I am myself now 14", she said, "and it is time for my own sacrifice and entry into the goddess's kingdom. I look forward longingly to my sacrificial day. I want to be accepted into the realm of love where I will be happy with our goddess, and I will never be lonely again.

"On the day of my sacrifice, I bathe for a very long time. I am given a bowl of a gelatin with something in it to relieve the pain of the sword.

"At the altar, I pray for the last time to our goddess. 'Goddess of Love, I am ready. I hope I have served you truly and loyally. Accept me as your servant.'

"The new Dancer performs the Dance of Love for our goddess. Then it is time for my sacrifice. I take the sword and thrust it into my chest, but it doesn't go in as far as I had hoped. It is difficult to stab yourself in the chest, I discover. Now I am in shock. I feel my warm blood spilling out of my body, and I see my successor catching it in the bowl. There's a throbbing pain in my heart and lungs.

"I seem to be stuck between two worlds, and now my soul can't go forward or back into my dying body. Darkness descends. Where is the goddess? She is nowhere. I wish I could become alive again, but I know I can't go back. Now I realize everything was an illusion, even the goddess whom I served so loyally. We had been deceived, all of us. All those rituals and sacrifices couldn't save the world, I now knew. We only brought death to all those pretty, little girls.

"Slowly, I leave my body. I can see the new dancer drinking my blood, while my successor watches. I want to tell them it's no use. There is neither goddess nor eternal life, but they can't hear me."

It had been a long session, and Gina was very tired. They decided to look back later as to what they had uncovered from this life experience.

"After regressions," says Ingrid," the soul knows far more than it did when it was earthbound. Everything becomes clear to it."

Several days later, Ingrid and Gina met again.

"What was behind this life experience, Gina?" Ingrid asked as they began the session. "Well, I know that this period was before Greece was founded," the young woman said. She explained that from what she had learned in that life, there were people from the West who had invaded the country. They wanted to introduce different gods, and they also wanted to conquer and completely subjugate these people. They brought in this goddess worship by promising to stop suppression and misery. The goddess was also expected to bring peace and harmony to the country. Before she came to be worshiped, there had been famine, war and hatred.

The secret agenda of this Western group of people, however, was to keep the country's population from increasing. More children would produce more warriors.

The temple to the goddess was built, and people were encouraged to bring their daughters to serve the goddess. They weren't told, of course, of the fate that awaited them there. Other girls were kidnapped and brought to the priestesses for sacrifice.

The temple and its goddess existed for 30 years. Thousands of young girls were sacrificed to her during that time.

Gina remembered the name of the goddess. It sounded like Cory, she said.

Some time later, Ingrid's interest in the chilling story caused her to look up the name "Cory." What she found was "Kore," an archaic name for Persephone, daughter of Demeter, goddess of agriculture. The two were very involved with the still unknown Elysium Mysteries. The Elysium Fields was the home of the blessed after death.

According to legend, Demeter was grief stricken when Kore was kidnapped by Hades, the god of the underground, and made his bride. The mother wandered the world till she found her daughter. During that time, nothing grew on the Earth. After she found Kore with Hades, Demeter begged him to release her daughter. He did so, but he gave his bride a pomegranate seed to eat. Because of that, Kore was allowed to remain with her mother part of the year, during Earth's growing season, but she returned to her husband during what became winter.

Could Gina's strange past life be associated in any way with these Elysium Mysteries?

Ingrid notes that Gina's regression experiences were rather typical. Many of them show how God - or a goddess - was portrayed, she says.

"No one really knows God, but many say they do. Some do terrible things in their god's name. The true story is that such excesses are always really political in nature.

"It also reflects that part of human nature that always seeks liberation, freedom, eternal life, and high values. Somewhere inside us, we know that the soul is eternal. It is always dissatisfied with the world as it appears.

"The soul seeks to establish eternal truths, and that can't be done by institutions or authority but by inviting our inner nature to reveal itself to us.

"All this striving for power lies in man's attempts to establish true inner power rather than the unstable outer power. I have discovered that much sorrow in this world is caused by us looking for good things in the wrong places. For example, we go to war to establish outer power or we take drugs to temporarily soothe the quest for peace and harmony, only to become addicted to them."

Since Gina had been put in the temple involuntarily in that long ago life, she became a victim. Hers was a life of effect and not of cause.

A further regression with Gina revealed a life of a woman whose husband ruled a land, probably somewhere in ancient or Medieval Europe. She was not happy with this husband and decided to get rid of him and claim the kingdom for herself. With the help of a corrupt priest, she did just that. She and the priest made a criminal pact that he would have the power of the church and she the worldly power.

Soon, they carried out their evil plan. With her husband dead, she came to power as planned. While he had been a just ruler, she was unjust and cruel. She raised an army to conquer more territory and raised taxes to pay for it. When her people protested, she told them she was doing it all for them so their country would be richer and more powerful. She was extravagant, indulging in feastings and other pleasures.

"I wear beautiful, long velvet gowns in rich brown and red colors, encrusted with jewels, and my hair is beautifully groomed and tied with ribbons," Gina said.

"My clothes are sometimes made of a golden fabric, too, and I wear many jewels."

She decided to enlarge her kingdom through wars, but she was so arrogant that her counselors warned her she was going too far. When she discussed how best to conquer a neighboring country, one counselor suggested she marry the ruler of the next country rather than fight him.

"Marry him indeed?" she asked scornfully. "I prefer to conquer him."

She lost the ensuing battle in what Gina perceived to be primitive warfare. She was then brought before her enemy. He offered to marry her.

"I would rather lose everything than marry you," she told him.

He happily obliged her. Her fate was to be entombed alive standing in a wall where she lingered without food or water for almost two weeks. Her death was very painful. Gina shuddered as she recalled worms and beetles invading her skin and the ants which explored her ears.

The priest came to the wall where she was entombed one day and cursed her, saying "You will never get out - you will be trapped in the void. You will forget everything, and if you try to remember, you will fall into a depth and be stuck there eternally. The pain will be so bad you'll crave non existence and wish you'd never been born - if someday you try to progress and develop, you'll never get anywhere. All is futile."

Looking back on that life after she came out of regression, Gina said, "I was not willing to compromise and I was so arrogant that I sacrificed thousands of lives."

"I had no reason to kill all those people, and as I died I resolved to be humble and of service to others in other lives."

Apparently that priest of that far off lifetime is her half brother in this current life, says Ingrid.

"They get along very well now, but that's not so surprising," says Ingrid."After all, they were both guilty of so many things, including murder, in their past. Thus it is their destiny to support and defend each other through many lifetimes. She has helped him financially, and no one in their family dares interfere with their relationship."

Her successful explorations of her past lives released Gina of the fears that had plagued her, and she went on to successfully complete her naturopath exam and renew her zest for life.

She assures Ingrid that she never studied history prior to these regressions. In fact, she wasn't even interested in the past. Since learning of the regressions, her brother became very interested in visiting Rome's catacombs as well as viewing a black book said to be in the Vatican's library.

Ingrid recently asked Gina how she felt about her regression experience. "I feel that the major help was to learn that the soul is immortal," she said.

"Those curses the priest placed upon me have been lifted through regression, and I truly feel I can now accomplish something with this life. I can handle my problems by listening to the inner truths, and I stick to my own opinions rather than let someone else inflict theirs on me.

"I would like others to know that these regressions were a lot for me to grasp, but within two years of completing them, everything changed in my life. My mother no longer is able to dominate me because I understand her. And I know finally why my father was so cold to me all those years, so I don't suffer any more from that. My marriage is getting better all the time; in fact, my whole life has turned around."

Gina became so interested in past life regression that she studied it under Ingrid and is now one of her therapists. Gina worked on regressions with her sister, and they slowly uncovered the secrets of their past.

Gina's is only one of thousands of similar case histories in Ingrid's files of past life regressions. She explains that everyone is somewhat alike, yet as different as the snowflakes that cover the Northern lands in the winter.

"Sometimes we experience rather tranquil lives while others may be tragic. One time, we may be the victim and in another the victimizer. It is those trauma-filled lives that often leave us with the scars that follow us lifetime after lifetime.

"Our freedom of choice is restored once we face down and resolve those bad choices we made in some of our past lives."

CHAPTER 20

RESOLVING THOSE "FATAL FLAWS"

Ingrid explains that the findings and contents of regression work confirms some belief systems, but on the other hand surpasses many boundaries of thought.

"My studies with regression have yet to reveal any theories such as 'a thousand consecutive lifetimes spent as a plant or animal.' I do get occasional revelations that our souls may possibly have had some experiences in the past as plants and animals. This is especially true when I regress children. Children have no ego yet, so they have no trouble with going back to the mineral/plant level.

"There may even have been some point when our souls were encased in stones, staying there until the stone was crushed or until the soul decided to move out. A wild idea? Perhaps, but who are we to judge what is or isn't possible in this strange universe in which we survive life after life?

"I am very open to all belief systems, for I subscribe to no one theory of life," she says.

Sometimes Ingrid will ask a client to go back to Earth's beginnings. She'll say "What kind of animal, plant and mineral do you relate to and to which don't you relate?" By this method, she says, we learn that particular soul's first incarnation on this planet. It seems that it took eons before the soul entered Earth's plane.

Since regression work is a very profound approach, getting to the root of human behavior, she sees her clients experience deep set changes in personality, moods and even motivation.

"It seems our original programming keeps us going. It motivates us in our goals as well as to incarnate over and over again," she explains.

"When you touch on these underlying programs that have been carried over so many lifetimes, you render them transparent, and their influence on the person fades away. It's rather like an engine that's been running for a long time and is suddenly stopped. It may wonder what else there is to do in life than to pursue a certain path."

She says that we have been functioning for so long based on these programs that when these are questioned, there is a lack of assignment.

"This can make anyone moody and seemingly without purpose for awhile. It's a healthy process to step back and look at 'what makes life tick,' and not to perpetuate or engage in the same routines over and over. This stage will fade, allowing the client to reassert control over life.

"The difference is that now the goals are voluntarily decided upon. The new activities are now of free will, not fueled by old behaviors. This way, a new type of freedom is experienced."

She goes on to say that most clients who have undergone thorough regression work describe this feeling as having 'a new beginning' or a 'new life.'

"There have always been so much death and violence on this planet where we kill to eat and survive. No other planet has such a bloody history as ours. On higher evolved worlds, they use more gentle forms of energy. Yes, by our biology humans are very primitive creatures on this planet and some of us remain even more so.

"Ours, however, is a very rich planet that is currently in a strong span of technical and spiritual development. Souls flock here to take part in it, for the type of experience on Earth ranges from primitive culture to space technology. That's one reason why there now is an overpopulation of humans. Everyone wants to experience what's happening here."

Ingrid adds that when we regress past our recent lives, we may go further back in time. Some people she has regressed remember lives on other planets which is why she believes Earth is not the first stage of our souls' evolution but rather a late stage. Lives on other planets are interesting in that the process of life and death may vary greatly. Morals, laws, regulations and lifestyles differ very much from that of Earth. Past life work broadens the spectrum tremendously, and limitations in thinking are dissolved.

She asks, "Have you noticed how Science always seems to lag behind? It will first deny and then, years later confirm, truths long known by the mystical world. This is also true with genetic research. In regression, we have long known that Earth has been visited by extra terrestrials and that the human race is a genetic manipulation of visitors from outer space.

"How else could you explain that nature took millions of years to evolve the animals and plants but modern man emerged only between 10,000 and 50,000 years ago and multiplied into all our different races? Now, with all the genetic findings, it's clear that the body of the human species is made up of biological genes, not of chemicals."

Ingrid points out that there are plants that apparently originated in certain places on Earth, such as corn or maize, but have genes that may have come from outer space. These genes are to be found nowhere else on Earth. This confirms that the subconscious with its "memories" is much more on the track and more reliable than sheer logical science."

Why do so many past lives seem to be full of trauma? Well, actually they're not, she says. Positive and negative experiences aren't viewed in proportion, one for one. Ten positive experiences often won't outweigh one negative one. You could, for example, be on a two week vacation. The first week and five days could have been wonderful, but on the sixth day you somehow break your leg! You feel the whole vacation was a disaster! You've forgotten the twelve wonderful vacations days and focus on the unlucky thirteenth one.

She goes on to say that past life work often seems to handle negative incidents, but by the nature of negative incidents, these have to be taken care of before the positive experiences of that life can emerge.

Ingrid points out that "we wouldn't feel any negativity if we had no comparison to positive experiences. We've lived many positive lifetimes, as well as those that were mediocre or simply boring. I tend to compare the different lifetimes to the days of our current lives.

Remember all the many days we live through without being able later to recollect them?

"We only remember outstanding events, such as weddings, parties, childbirth, rewards, promotions, political events, accidents, disappointments, deaths and losses."

At the same time, she says, it is not at all necessary for us to cover many lifetimes but rather to access those key incidents in our past lives. They are the ones influencing this life.

The other important issue is that past life therapy simplifies and reduces the different aspects of problems to one core issue. So, even if you do not wish to access earlier lives, you can find your underlying troubles with a direct and straightforward technique. This is the karmic task in the core issue that governs each of our lives.

"Much psychotherapy will treat various symptoms but they do not always touch the core issue," she says, stressing that "with past life techniques, we always focus on the core issue of one lifetime. When we know this underlying task, we can use our new insight as a guideline in making decisions."

CHAPTER 21

Margo and Dieter Were Soul Mates

Margo and Dieter came into Ingrid's life through one of her seminars. Actually she met Dieter there. He was in his 30's at that time. She noticed him that day because he was one of those people who always look down and never gaze at the lecturer. He appeared withdrawn from the other students.

When they reached the section in which they dealt with the origin of these difficulties, he finally looked up, and she saw that his eyes were a deep blue.

"I have a problem," he volunteered. "Well, tell me what it is."

"I'm stuck in an accident from outer space," he said.

He appeared to be serious about it. Ingrid thought how peculiar that this shy man would come out with an outer space incident and decided to do a "problem analysis" with him. He came up with an image of having had a spacecraft accident. In it, he'd been pulled into space. During this experience, he never knew if he were dead or alive or even if he were in or out of his body.

He said he seemed to float through different worlds.

"I feel as if I'm an alien to this planet," he said.

Dieter, it turned out, was a very talented artist. This space accident event had haunted and inspired him all his life. The image they brought forth, however, of being lost and wandering in space was new to him.

The exercise seemed to help him ground himself, for after that he began paying attention to our seminar.

When they met, they were on one of those week long vacation seminars which Ingrid gave in Switzerland that year. Although lots of classes were offered, the attendees also had the opportunity for hiking and other free time activities.

Ingrid saw Dieter quite often that week and found him to be rather a strange, intense man with "different" channels of perception. Ordinary conversations were difficult for him.

She was surprised and pleased when, at their last night Gala, he gave her one of his paintings. It had unusual reincarnation overtones. When they talked afterwards, he showed her his catalogue of pictures. All seemed to have an outer space theme, and they were very good. They were professional in quality, as clear as photographs.

"These belong in a museum, Dieter," Ingrid told him. "Or, better yet, perhaps the Stuttgart Planetarium."

The world famous planetarium is noted for its art shows. Dieter agreed he would like to exhibit there, and she said she would contact the Planetarium for him which she did a few days later. While artists usually must wait up to seven years for an exhibit slot, Dieter's work was so exceptional that the officials decided to put his exhibit in as soon as possible. His exhibition opened there within the year.

About that time, Dieter introduced Ingrid to his wife, Margo. Around 30 years old and petite, she had dark, short hair and blue eyes. Her features were very Egyptian. With a start of surprise, Ingrid realized that she had seen her face before - in Dieter's paintings. He told her he'd been painting that face for years before he met his wife.

"When I met Margo, I realized she was the woman I had been painting all of my life," he confessed.

And Margo said that she, too, had felt a rush of recognition when she first saw him.

She told Ingrid that she had seen Dieter from behind, and knew immediately "that's my husband."

Margo decided to go into regression with Ingrid. Her past revealed one life in which she was an herb woman. A man she treated with these herbs died, and she was burned at the stake. He died because she couldn't admit she didn't know how to cure him.

Even in the dark ages, when outwardly prejudice and misconceptions prevailed, the inner law of cause and effect remained intact. Sometimes what seems to be an injustice is the consequence of an earlier action. You can be judged in one life for something you did in a former life.

Margo spent another life as a man. This time, she was an overseer for a land owner somewhere in Europe. Her persona in this life received bribes and presents from the peasants. She asked for more and more bribes, and the people hated her. Later in that life she became addicted to alcohol and died.

And then they uncovered her life in Egypt.

"I'm a priestess. I have been educated to be a channel for our goddess Isis. I spend years in this education and then, just when I'm about to assume my duties, I give it all up for a relationship with the high priest. Oh, it's Dieter. I have to have him. But then I'm found out. I'm losing my powers. Everything I trained for. I begin taking drugs. Now all is lost, all!"

This appeared to be the theme of Margo's lives. She always strived for success then sabotaged it.

With any client, after doing several regressions with different types of lives, you can usually find the deep, core issue involved with a problem. Some traumas can be so buried that it takes several regressions to uncover them. Margo's underlying issue was "success will make me arrogant. I'll abuse my power, and people will die of my hand, therefore I will sabotage success"

The breakthrough came during her fourth regression. During this lifetime, Margo was born into a simple family. Later she joined a religious group of people. She admired the group leader and rose through the ranks. Some years later, the leader died and she assumed command. She quickly became cruel and demanding. Her followers were ordered to collect taxes. She sold daughters of her workers to wealthy traders. Her followers tried to warn her that she was not following the teachings of the original leader, but she ignored them.

"One of my most trusted confidantes comes to me to warn me that my life is in danger. I ask him 'what can I do?' And he tells me to follow him. We go to some woods. What? No!

There are others from our group here. They want to kill me because I'm so cruel. He kills me. It's all over.

In other regressions, they kept finding this same pattern. In one, Margo was the wife of a rich man who traveled a lot. Again, her husband was Dieter. Someone came to her while he was gone and told her she was a chosen one. Intrigued, she joined what turned out to be a coven.

There, she was initiated and taken into an elite group.

Her task was to bring in money. She sold jewelry and objects from her home. When her husband discovered what was happening, he went to the coven and told them to leave her alone. He no longer respected her, however, and she spent the rest of her life atoning for the experience by becoming a servant. In this lifetime, Margo realized, she got into trouble because she was looking for excitement and thought she needed something outside to get it.

Another lifetime found her a married woman who started an affair to make her husband jealous. He threw her out and she ended up an alcoholic living in a poorhouse.

They had found the pattern. In each life, Margo lived good lives until she ruined them by her own actions. It was her fatal flaw to believe that "there's no point in success because you lose it anyway."

Although she worked extraordinarily hard for success, in the end it seemed she found it to be a kind of freedom to be able to destroy what she had created. Her lives were a series of taking big steps to the top, staying there for a short while, only to topple back down.

She did it to show herself that she could succeed at anything. Then she would destroy it, rather like a child at the beach building sandcastles only to tear them back down.

Regressions reveal the personality very quickly, like a magnifying glass reflecting the soul's structure and its underlying subtle programming.

Ingrid once asked Margo what she thought her regressions had done for her.

After a moment's thought, she said, "Without past life therapy, how could I have ever gotten out of this cycle of always creating and then destroying?"

The stressess and issues uncovered by Margo's regressions come from a past steeped in magic and priestly incarnations. Such oaths are a source of suggestion to the soul. There is the oath, the Master, a source of information, authority, the presence of the gods and the priesthood. All are manipulations of mystical encounters, for you can program the soul to believe anything, if the authority is strongly portrayed and endowed with powers and if the soul thinks its obedience is for its own spiritual growth and that it's for its own good.

Even in this life, Margo was sowing the same kind of traumas she'd had in previous lifetimes. For example, she had contemplated an affair to make Dieter more interested in her, and she was subtly hurting his career by making fun of him. Her attitude said "I do whatever I want."

Margo, however, sincerely wanted to break her core life pattern, once she became aware of it. You have to be sincere in therapy and find those weaknesses and bad parts and face them. Once you see your pattern and understand it, then you can terminate it by fixing it. You don't just handle the symptoms.

Today, Margo is doing very well. She is a part time therapist who is building a strong client list. Once more, she is on the road to success, but this time, with her new knowledge, she won't self destruct.

If you take part in a regression, the experience will expose the underlying incident of some problem in your past, but the key to solving the issue is to understand and link it to your present life. It is important to grasp the inner meaning of your experience, or it will once again sink back into your subconscious. This change in your present life will come about when you analyze and evaluate your new knowledge. You can then ask yourself "What did I learn and what should I have done differently that I can use to change now?"

Regression can be dangerous under certain circumstances, warns Ingrid. If the therapist doesn't allow the client to relive all the content of the regression or later analyze the experience, it is like an open wound to your psyche. Past lives have only been stirred up and not resolved by those problems you have uncovered.

If you go into regression, says Ingrid, plan to accept the responsibility for what you uncover. The question to be asked after every each one is "What is the lesson to be learned from this?" The cause and effect law must be brought into this. For every life as a victim, you have lived one as a victimizer. You must uncover both lives, no matter how many regressions it takes.

Gina, the young woman who remembers being a dancer/high priestess for the goddess Kore, had five regressions before they discovered all the pieces of her puzzle. And Margo had seven or eight.

The purpose of therapy is to find a clear picture of that soul's past lives. Each regression shows us a piece of the puzzle, but it takes up to eight regressions to reveal the core stress and to balance out all our major personal issues.

For example, if you were a fanatic in one lifetime, why were you? Obviously, your answer lies in another lifetime where you may have ignored or downplayed that same issue causing you to become a fanatic later. The objective for each of us is to resolve the dilemmas, no matter how long it takes.

As in psychology analyses, not resolving your problems, leaving them hanging, can be dangerous for you. Don't stir up your past and not handle what you find there.

Of course, opening one door and finding something that distresses you may lead to your opening several other doors, but there's no need to become discouraged or frightened. Just follow the threads and they will lead you to all the pieces of your puzzle.

CHAPTER 22

ERIC AND KATJA

Eric did just that. He followed his threads. When Ingrid first met him, he had the weird idea that every woman who laid eyes on him immediately fell madly in love with him. She thought he looked like a monk, with his dark, short hair and his glasses. He was somewhere in his 20's at the time and an intern in a management company.

They met at a lecture on "How To Find Your Potential." He told Ingrid that he had studied engineering before taking his current position. Since he was interested in past life regression, he took her card and promised to call sometime.

As time went by, she heard from him occasionally. Once, he called to say he was taking a water therapy class. It was so nice, he said, that he was happy and he wanted to do that as a professional career. Ingrid advised him not to just jump into therapy work as a profession until he knew what he really wanted for a career.

"I want to work with people," he said.

Finally, he came in for his initial interview. That's when he told her his strange idea that every woman he met was in love with him.

"I'm afraid I sighed rather loudly at that one," says Ingrid with a laugh.

"Oh, but it's true. And if a woman quarrels with me or says 'no', well, it's just because she loves me so much," he told her.

He explained how, if a girl rejected him, he had to keep after her until she came around, but once that happened, he would immediately drop her. These brief affairs ended, however, before they became sexual. He just liked to play games.

There was a girl in his life, Katja whom he considered his one true love. He met her in school when he was a teenager. She was several years older and several grades ahead of him. He was very much in love with her but was always afraid to reveal this. She was very self assured, and he admired her. They dated for a while, but there was no intimacy. Both seemed to have a huge fear of rejection by the other. He introduced her to his parents, but his father didn't care for her.

Eric, however, was totally absorbed by Katja. What ruined their relationship was that every time one or the other attempted to openly show their love, the other would back off and act indifferent. The final end came when Katja attempted to bring their relationship closer. He, as usual, refused, and they split up. She moved away.

He later followed her to the town where she lived, several hundred miles away, only to discover that there were two names on the apartment bell, hers and a man's. But still, Eric couldn't stop thinking about Katja. He even told himself that she must have decided to live with another man in an attempt to forget their relationship.

During the first interview, he admitted he really wasn't too happy with his relationships and his unresolved career plans. He decided to begin regression work.

In an early regression, he found himself garbed as a knight in some medieval country. "I love the daughter of a king. I'm a knight trying to win her favor, but I'm a Casanova type, and she won't have anything to do with me. One day I regret living this superficial lifestyle. I tell her it's all a mistake, but she doesn't seem to care. I'm stubborn. I sulk and live alone.

Because I can't have her, I lose my career."

His remaining years in this life were spent in self pity for what he had lost. The princess, of course, was Katja.

Eric's problems seemed to revolve around a lack of closeness, intimacy and friendship.

This was further brought out in another lifetime. In this, his last life prior to the present, he was a powerful officer of the Third Reich. Women love him for this power. He has an intense social life. And then he again meets Katja.

This time, she's an imprisoned Jew. He takes her to be his maid and finds her to be pure. She is afraid of him. Because of their positions, he can't tell her of his affection. After the war ends, the prisoners capture and hang him. He understands why they do this and the last person he sees as he lies dying is his secret love, Katja.

"Now at death, I have this love connection, and I am as fragile as she is," he said sadly.

Political and traditional issues stood in their way during both of these lifetimes. This regression explained yet another recurring stress in his present life. He was afraid to speak to groups because of that hanging experience. Through this regression, he worked out his fears of public speaking. Terror of speaking in public often comes from being degraded, scorned, accused or sentenced in public.

Another of his regressions told of a life spent as a body slave to an Egyptian queen who liked having beautiful men as her personal slaves and lovers.

Eric is a beautiful man in this early life, with black hair and blue eyes. He has a bad habit of boasting about his sexual prowess. The Queen picks him out of a lineup of slaves and puts him in a dungeon for two months to build up his sexual urge. Then he is taken out, bathed and brought to the queen.

Unfortunately, he can't perform as expected, so she kicks him out. Now he is used as a sexual object by men and women who are into kinky sex. He becomes mentally disturbed and dies six years later. His soul decides it's had enough of sex for eternity.

The sex wasn't really the problem there, points out Ingrid. On a personal level he failed because he first bragged about his potency and how strong and masculine he was. Politically, he failed because he could have played a role in linking the master and the slave classes of this society. Vanity made him fail.

Another lifetime found him in South Africa as a member of a white colonial family. He broke that society's cultural taboos by having an affair with a black maid. His father took him to Vienna, supposedly on vacation but actually to imprison him in a psychiatric hospital. The nurses were sadistic. They gave him electric shock treatments and beat him to rid him of "the devil." He died after two years of that "treatment."

"I betrayed my black love because I didn't stand up for her," he said. "I didn't treat her right."

He was cold and calculating in another lifetime spent in Europe. A pimp, he seduced women into falling in love with and becoming dependent on him. Then he'd turn them into prostitutes.

As Eric described it, "I'm the experienced man who knows what women want. I'm a good lover. They all feel special and they stay with me forever.

"Whoever falls in love with me is lost, for I use it and feed on it."

This was the key to all his games, and it was also reflected in his current life. Now he was holding women off because he didn't want to hurt them.

In this earlier life of being a pimp, Katja again entered his world. This time she was a highly born lady. He fell in love with her because she was the one woman he couldn't manipulate. This time he destroyed their relationship by telling her about his way of life. She left him and disappeared. Soon, he lost everything, including his life.

This time, said Eric, "I lost the chance to win the one woman in my life because I hadn't enough courage to make it without macho power in back of me."

"In every life, there is a turning point where we can change everything around," says Ingrid, "but this has a price. You may have to give up a comfortable life style and/or start a new one you haven't tried before. If that life change is missed or botched, things get difficult and deteriorate quickly. This was Eric's problem in his chain of lives."

According to Ingrid Vallieres' case files, Eric also experienced being female in other lives. In one he found himself living as "Jacqueline" in a Western saloon in the United States sometime in the 19th Century.

Jacqueline grew up in New Orleans before heading for the gold fields of the Old West. A dancer and singer, she was a beautiful woman with many admirers. One day while taking a bath, she was raped by a stranger. He called her a prostitute and threatened to kill her. The experience changed Jacqueline, and she turned against men. After that, she tried to dominate them by using her sexuality to gain power over them. She wasn't close to anyone. Instead, she became a madam of a brothel. She died at 40, an acute alcoholic.

Eric learned during the course of his regressions that the game he played was that he was the "unsolvable mystery." He lived behind a mask, and the game entailed wondering how long it would take people to understand that he lived a different life on the inside.

He now understands he is afraid to have a relationship with the soul that was Katja and the Princess because he's afraid she, too, will remember their past. He's afraid he will again jeopardize or mess up their relationship one more time.

In his subconscious, he feels as long as he doesn't get close to any woman, he'll be safe.

The name of the game is pretend interest but don't get involved.

"In Eric, we see the polarity of the tough guy on the outside, hungry for real life on the inside," says Ingrid. "Sometimes such people fall into an authoritarian mode, yet they long for love. I'm happy to say he's worked out his problems. He has dropped his masks and is unafraid of his emotions."

Will he finally win his Katja? It's not important. The main thing is that he finally understands all the pieces of his puzzle. He is now more open and sincere in his relationships. He's lost his fear of commitment and the need to hide his weaknesses. He has engaged in emotional and sexual relationships and experienced a closeness never known to him before. The whole area of relationships turned out to be very rewarding. Today, he is a therapist along with his management position. Overcoming his fear of commitment has allowed him to come closer to people who need his help. He has fathered a son and published several books on spirituality.

In regression, explains Ingrid, you must be willing to work with the unknown. Once you open the door to new insights, you may become vulnerable. If you find that your self image was based on unreal or unethical attitudes, it may cost you your illusions. There will be no solutions until you say goodbye to certain habits. Your reward will be a healthier and stronger self image and personality.

Another therapist once told Ingrid about a client who came in for a regression. She was a proud woman who was in the middle of rather a frivolous law suit because she was sure she was right. It had to do with her belief that she was wronged in another life and now she would be victorious in this.

When she was regressed, it turned out that she had been the victimizer in that other life, not the victim. Because she no longer felt victimized, she decided to drop her lawsuit. So, sometime what you find out during a regression may be a surprise to you and change your attitudes. Things that once loomed as problems no longer seem important.

"Whenever you open yourself to change, some things will be taken away, but you will gain the truth" says Ingrid, "you won't rest until you learn the truth."

Truth will always resolve the problem and bring about relief. Conversely, hiding from it only prolongs misery.

Our freedom of choice is returned to us with the truth. We became the victim of bad choices in the past. Once we resolve these, we have the freedom to choose better options.

"I find we have so much experience, we have lived so many lifetimes, that not to take the opportunity to learn from them is a waste. We can take the knowledge and turn it into pure gold," Ingrid stresses.

CHAPTER 23

GARY'S STORY

In studying our past lives, if we can understand our past misfortunes, we can turn that knowledge into our good fortune in this present life, Ingrid reports.

"That desire to go back and do it over again is possible in that we can learn from it, clean it up and change our ways. Even those who don't or can't believe in the possibility of reincarnation want a second chance, too. Those who say they don't believe, really do. But they don't want to face their past unfortunate choices," she explains.

A young man named Gary was like that. Ingrid remembers the first time she met him. He was tall, handsome, with bright brown eyes and light red hair. He had a radiant smile. Surely such a confident appearing, sturdy young man couldn't have serious problems? But he did.

"I'm so depressed," he told her.

As Ingrid has often noted, although a client may seem radiant and positive when she meets him, it is possible that inside he feels weak and insecure. And, conversely, those who appear the weakest and most insecure actually can have an inner core of strength.

"I have discovered through my years of therapy that apparently contradictory inward and outward attitudes are caused by unresolved past life issues," she says. "The outer appearance of a person may relate to one lifetime while the way he or she feels inwardly may relate to another. In that latter life he was outwardly confident, but the inner lack of confidence comes from a more hopeless lifetime.

"People seeing only the exuberant outer personality often won't take complaints of unhappiness seriously."

Gary, she learned, was this type of personality. Ingrid began a series of regressions with him to discover the root of his pain.

"I guess my biggest problem right now is that I love luxury. In fact, I love the good life so much I'm head over heels in debt," he said woefully.

"And I'm always having trouble with women. Everything starts great with a relationship and then it all falls apart on me."

"How about your business, your work?" she asked. "Oh, yeah, my business," he muttered.

"Yes?"

"That's another thing. Every time I go into business, it goes great for a while, and then I ruin it, one way or another."

No wonder Gary was depressed! Together they went through the usual regression through this life and prenatal experience and then back into his past lives. The breakthrough came in a life lived several thousand years ago.

"I'm a Roman ruler, a general, and I live in great luxury. Everyone admires me. I have everything - power, riches - and yet I'm not satisfied. I keep looking for more territory.

"So I sail to Egypt. The ruler there is a female. We meet, and she is the woman of my dreams. She is powerful in her own right. We appear exotic and powerful to each other, a strong aphrodisiac. Privately, we're so happy together. But her people won't accept me, and I'm getting reports that there is trouble in my own country.

"We talk about combining our two countries, but Rome refuses to consider the idea.

Curse the Senate! They're such fools! I hurry back to my country to explain my actions, and she will follow me there soon. But now, when I get to Rome, I find my people have turned against me because, they say, I'm partial to another country. They call me a traitor. And now they're killing me! What will I do without my Beloved?"

After this regression, Gary looked at Ingrid sadly. "Now I know why none of my relationships with women ever work out. I'm trying to find my dream woman in this lifetime, and what am I going to do if she's only in my past?"

Now, obviously, it was his present extravagant life style that was the big issue. What matters in the end is how you handled the important decisions in your life, as well as the dream mate and the missed successes of the past.

By living beyond his means, he was trying to recreate the setting of his previous powerful lifestyle. He hoped to get a second chance, but in reality he had neither the power nor the riches of that previous life nor did his dream woman appear. He, instead, failed at several business ventures.

The reason Gary subconsciously looked for this "dream woman" was because he regretted not handling his past life more successfully. The woman stood for hope, success and big goals as yet unrealized. His trouble in his present life was that, no matter how hard he tried, everything slipped through his hands. This was not a coincidence but his subconscious was trying to tell him to be more responsible, mature and diplomatic.

You see, if your ego realizes that you once muffed the chance of a lifetime to do something right, it will become determined to sabotage any future life's successes. It's still angry over the past failure, and it will punish you, making it all worse. Often such subliminal programming will contain subtle ways to ensure that we continue to punish ourselves and self- destruct lifetime after lifetime. Basically, it's a fear of taking on responsibilities and not being able to handle the good things of life and to make them last.

Gary's unhappiness turned out to be a very archetypical sequence of events. When you find repetitious bad things occurring in a life, you can be sure the problems arise from not handling something correctly in a past lifetime. Worse is that the constant failures can continue over a number of lifetimes, so it's important to examine their core and resolve it now.

Ingrid explains that the archetypical sequence of events means that first, we have "the chance of a lifetime" to do something beneficial for a large group of people. Secondly, that chance is mishandled. Usually this is due to shortsightedness and vanity in which one tends to overlook vital details. Thirdly, if it fails, it will bring on the regret and subsequential perpetuation of self punishment and failure.

Underneath all this is the thought "if I couldn't handle this situation, then I'm not worthy of success."

The key incident occurs when everything is open to the soul. It is still forming its karma. This big opportunity doesn't come very often during our lifetimes and when it does, it's a "key incident." How we handle this key incident will be reflected in lifetimes to come.

If we handle it well, we build up self confidence, knowledge and useful experience.

Handled badly, we go into self invalidations and failures.

Repeated failure, such as Gary experienced, isn't the only indication of such a karmic problem. There are also those who work all their lives for something and then, when they get it, they don't enjoy it. Or perhaps, somehow they just miss that success they've worked so hard for.

The wisdom gained from new understanding of you yourself more than pays for any loss of beliefs. The slate is wiped clean, the trauma is over, and any other distress can be handled as well. Gary had to make peace with the past, learn from it and let go of his punishment for his past failures to come to appreciate what he has in his present life.

"I know that it can be frightening to realize the vast implications of cause and effect and how your choices in the past still haunt you," says Ingrid. "And it can be even more frightening to decide to change, but if you don't integrate your new knowledge into this life, the same situations once faced before will occur again and again. If you don't get any new insight, you can't change your life pattern. The good news is that with new insights, you can change any life pattern."

In every regression, the solution is to find out why you are sabotaging yourself and to learn how to avoid doing this. Might you be secretly afraid of success? Do you really want it? Do you believe you're worth it or is there a hidden clause in your subconscious telling you that no, you don't deserve it? Once you know the truth, the truth will set you free. Remember, if you always do what you always did, you will always get what you always got.

CHAPTER 24

WE ARE THE SUM OF ALL OUR LIVES

What happened in our past lives is often reflected in our present. The irrational fears and the traumas can be resolved through therapy. You don't have to suffer from the past.

There are a number of ways that regressions can be induced. While hypnosis is often thought to be the only method, actually it's not. Non hypnotic approaches are even more effective because these sessions allow you to settle naturally into regression. You don't have to be manipulated, either. The method Ingrid teaches never suggests. She asks you to look at and report what you see. You volunteer the possibilities yourself. As the therapist, she doesn't do this for you.

"We question; we do not suggest. This way you are totally free of manipulation. For example, I may ask a person who says he or she is on a battlefield who do they see. If they say "soldiers," the next question might be "what are they doing?" I might then ask what the scene looks like. Such experiences are relived through your own words, not that of me as your therapist."

Words, names, original names of a city, people or holy objects may come up. You may speak phrases of some ancient language, or perhaps you can read the sign above a temple or building. People experience regressions differently. Some are very visual and can explain what they see and experience in vivid detail. Others may talk more about their feelings. These sensory experiences differ from client to client.

Some of Ingrid's clients have even been able to read aloud texts they see in a regression, or they can explain details explicitly, as did Gina in her temple goddess regression.

Your emotions might be so intense you even cry while you go through a regression. You might even begin feel tears well up in your eyes when asked what would be your worst scenario. These tears may fall even before the picture comes to you, because your subconscious already knows. As your therapist, Ingrid wouldn't attempt to stop your emotional stress. She would just move on with the incident.

Have you ever had a recurring dream that always stops when the scenario becomes unpleasant? Or maybe it's just a dream that comes often to you, but you can't understand it. Often such dreams are trying to reveal a trauma or some bit of information about a past life. In regression, you can explore the meaning behind those haunting night visions.

For example, there are falling dreams in which you find yourself falling into an endless abyss. It is frightening when it occurs. You wake up sweating and grateful it was only a dream. All nightmares are past traumas. These falling dreams indicate you once fell off a cliff or high place to your death.

In another dream you find yourself being chased by someone or something. This may point to a past life when you were chased by a wild animal or enemies and killed.

Whatever your recurring dream is about, when you wake up try to finish the story your subconscious is trying to tell you. Use your imagination. What would be the worst case scenario and ending? Once you follow this technique to the end, you will find the nightmare will be gone.

One thing Ingrid has noticed over and over during regression is how time seems to go much faster for those involved. Sometimes you can lose all track of present time, for the subconscious is timeless. When you come out of regression, you realize how deeply you were immersed in your past. Even space seems to have no meaning, as you float in and out of faraway places and times.

When you identify a problem through your regression, you will be able to deal with it and it will cease to bother you. Realizing it will bring about the necessary change of thinking.

After all, if you throw a stone into a pool of water, that stone's descent will make ever widening rings, but then it disappears. And so do problems. They come, we handle them, they fade and then they are gone!. Our subconscious is like thick honey when a trauma is disclosed. It sinks through this honey-like substance, as we ponder about it. If we don't confront and handle it, the problem will remain there.

The Universe has never yet lost a problem! Whatever needs your attention will wait for you to solve it.

Sometimes we justify to ourselves this taking no action, but nothing is settled. The problem lies there, unchanged, and someday it will emerge again. It may reappear in this life or the next, for unless we deal with its ramifications, it remains with us always.

We each have a higher consciousness which is always present, especially after death. We need to learn to live at all levels of consciousness simultaneously. With meditation, we can rise above any past traumas for a while, but afterwards it still remains to trouble us.

We need the courage to do what we want to do and say "no" to what we don't want to do in this life.

A married woman might be miserable in her marriage, yet afraid to leave her husband. Instead, she dies of cancer. Illness is often an easy way out, especially cancer. If you say "I'd rather die than --," the message is received by your subconscious which then acts upon it. The subconscious is like a computer that stores everything, especially negative feelings and emotions.

Life has always been full of dangers, death and treachery, and our subconscious will put up a block to prevent an incident from a past life to again occur in this lifetime. It puts up its shield before you are attacked, for it will resist anything relating to deaths you have suffered in the past.

Interestingly, no past life problem will arise unless a similar situation has arisen in this present life. Our past lives receive permission from us to pop up so we are able to find the key to why it is with us today. Our subconscious has stored memories that can be triggered by events in our present lives. Thus, through visualization, tone, colors, buildings and places, it associates one event with another that may be long past. The trigger is always a sensory perception.

"Ten people may fear water, but all of them will fear it differently. When we ask what the trigger is for each fear, we learn these differences. It seems our subconscious acts as a trigger because it mixes past and present indiscriminately. The connecting spark, or common denominator, may be very simple. Since we can't analytically get into the subconscious, we must address it on a different level."

If you fear water, the triggers can be something like stepping out of your depth or losing sight of the horizon, and you panic. This is your trauma from a previous life coming to the surface.

Age can be a trigger. If you led a happy life until you were thirty. At that point, something terrible happened. Maybe there was a famine or a plague or war and many were killed. When in this present life you reach the age of thirty you may feel an unexplainable depression or deep sadness where before you always had a positive outlook on life. You never know what will kick in from a past life experience.

No matter what is your age, you will always use the same solution to solve a problem unless you learn a new way to do this. Forgetfulness in old age can mean that there remain dilemmas that weren't dealt with in this current life. No one wants to die, yet the subconscious can convince us it's the only solution. It doesn't know of a better one. This is especially true when a similar situation has led to death before.

In the case of suicide, people see killing themselves as a solution because in a past life the same incidents brought about death. A wrong decision in a past life may have led to abandonment, failure and finally death.

You see, we are the total sums of all our past lives. All the patterns of our present life go back to the beginning of our lifetime in the prenatal and birth areas. These in turn act as a trigger for our past life patterns.

Looking for the trigger of a symptom or unwanted condition is the detective part of being a past life therapist. Once found, the past will open like a rose and all will be revealed. It is as much a revelation for the client as it is for the therapist.

CHAPTER 25

BEAUTY ISN'T EVERYTHING

As Ingrid points out, for every recurring problem, there is a fully fledged past life at the cause.

"I'm reminded about beautiful Renata who came to me because she seemed to always have everything go wrong for her after they always started so well.," she says.

She describes 28 year old Renata as being tall, with black, naturally curly hair, blue eyes and a winning smile.

"I need help desperately," Renata blurted out when they met.

Ingrid wondered what could be wrong in the life of this young woman, with her cover girl looks.

"I've done it again. I've blown it, and now I've lost the man of my dreams," Renata wailed, sitting across from her in her office in Stuttgart.

Ingrid handed her a tissue, which she dabbed at her eyes rather dramatically. "Really?"

"Yes, really," she replied, before adding in a bitter voice, "But then, I should have expected it. Everything was going so well, just like it always does at first, and then I blew it, just like I always do!"

Ingrid found that Renata was a popular woman with many friends, but somehow she was afraid of commitment and drove away those who loved her the most. She agreed to help the other woman find the seat of her difficulty. It proved to be an interesting discovery.

Renata began her story. "I'm the mistress of a king. We're French. I did something terrible in my past and now I'm being blackmailed over this by some people. I'm a psychic, and the blackmailer is using me as a channel to tell bad things to clients. These clients are usually women. I tell them horrible visions and I curse them, for I don't believe in happiness. It never lasts and ends terribly, I tell them. I'm leading a double life. I meet these people at night. It's a magical circle designed to control people. I go into a trance for them. All those curses I put on others are coming back on me."

Since in this past life, Renata had destroyed the happiness of many people, separating numerous couples and sowing the seeds of doubt and mistrust, her Karmic conscience was blocking her own happiness and relationships.

"Renata relived several other lives before finding the peace she was seeking," says Ingrid." We undid all the curses that she had thrown on others which came back on her in this lifetime. Thus we restored her own control of her life."

The law of cause and effect is universal: what you do unto others will be done unto you. You may even do it to yourself. Putting curses on others is an indication of the fear of being dominated and a feeling of powerlessness. It seems to be the universal task of every being on Earth to discover one's true power and to try to develop it. Those working on the tasks given them by a higher power have a more natural relationship with others. Fear is always an indication we are neglecting what we were placed here to do.

Bridget and her sons were a different story, says Ingrid.

Do you have a favorite saying? Bridget did. Hers was "the universe doesn't care about me."

Bridget, 43 and prematurely gray-haired, was a school teacher who had recently divorced a psychotic man. He only wanted to be served, and he completely dominated her when they were together. He made many demands of her. One was that she serve whatever he said his needs were any time of the day and night. She came to Ingrid to learn why she had permitted such a person to have control over her.

In her regressions, Bridget found one lifetime in which she was banished to an island to die of thirst. She had been exiled by her husband in that life because she was considered too rebellious and independent with political ideas. When she was dying of thirst, she cried out "the universe doesn't care about me." This was the same favorite complaint she had in her present life.

Interestingly, when she came in for that session she was very thirsty, and she had to drink a great deal of water.

Further regressions revealed that she had very close connections to her two sons of this lifetime. All three of them underwent regressions subsequently.

Aaron, Bridget's 16-year-old son, had acne. His prenatal regression revealed that his father questioned his mother if it was his child and this created a sense of rejection for the as yet unborn boy. Such skin problems as acne often indicate a desire to keep others away.

In another regression, Bridget was a powerful duke, her husband was a black magician who helped the Duke stay in power by destroying those who got in their way. He dominated the Duke who voluntarily entered into the symbiotic relationship. The helper was first killed by the magician and the Duke and they, in turn, were later killed by a rival ruler seeking their power who in this life turned out to be her husband. She tried subconsciously to keep out any disagreements to protect the family. In this past life, her eldest son was her magician husband and her younger son was their helper whom they murdered. The rival ruler was her present day husband.

Her two sons hated and loved each other in this lifetime, yet they were always together because of the symbiosis in the background. They felt they had to stick together.

"We had first opened the door on their troubled past," says Ingrid, "and now we followed through to reach a conclusion that would bring them peace and relieve their continuing tensions from those other lives."

She explains that when we unleash hidden truths during regression, we must always follow through with the process of coming to a full understanding of any ramifications.

Self discovery and self realization is a central theme of all psychologists, sociologists and educational theorists. Everyone agrees it's difficult for anyone to find him or herself. Why is this true? Does it come from inside ourselves or does it erupt from things that happen to us in this life? We can't find ourselves, if we don't seek our true selves first. We remain stuck in previous roles with certain people we know in this life.

Ingrid reports that while it may seem hard to believe, there are those who live all their lives without ever asking "who am I, really?" Such people often seem quite innocently at ease with themselves without ever questioning their own identities. We aren't just the person whose life we're currently leading; we are a culmination of all the lives we've led. Remnants of those past lives can enhance or disturb our present life. It's important to learn to distinguish between our present thoughts and emotions and remnants of a previous life.

CHAPTER 26

REGRESSION BEGINS

Ingrid begins each course of reincarnation therapy with a preliminary talk. From this she obtains a picture of your life situation. Important points are the experiences of childhood and your relationship with your parents and siblings. The nature of these interactions reflects past roles.

Conflicts and difficulties in your childhood are direct pointers to corresponding event in your earlier lives. Such difficulties might include taking offence easily, shyness or aggression. Or they might include the death of a parent, the effects of war or other tragic circumstances. In reincarnation therapy, Ingrid as therapist and you as client proceed from the assumption that your present childhood is a continuation of your former lives. Anything not worked through in the past will be encountered again in childhood.

Operations and accidents are important because statements made by doctors and nurses while you're under anesthetic go unfiltered directly to the subconscious. This suggestive material must sometimes be made conscious before regression into your former lives can begin. Such suggestions as "It's all in vain," or "We're not making any progress," for example can give you the feeling in every session that there's no point in this therapy and that you aren't making any progress. Only when these blocks are removed can there be open entry into your subconscious.

Your interactions with your marriage partner and the opposite sex in general give Ingrid an idea about your personality and about possible difficulties that might arise. Some have intimate relationships that always end the same way and faced with the same problems. In such a case, there is something that needs to be worked out.

When you choose the same type of person for a relationship time after time it offers a clear picture of your personality. For example, says Ingrid, if a woman always chooses dominating men who want to rule her life, it's quite possible she's trying to work out the issue of control and domination from a past life in order to learn from it.

Tragic losses, such as death of a loved one or a separation, may indicate that in past lives you also suffered heavy losses. They recur when in this lifetime similar tragedies make the loss even more painful. Losses can counteract life's good times because we will remember the losses and sorrows far more than the happy occurrences in our lives.

Everything you encounter continuously in this life and find hard to bear are signs of past experiences which haven't been pleasant. Both birth and death can be uncomfortable experiences.

In regression, Ingrid closely watches the tone of voice, body language and physical tensions of her client. These indicate the gravity of the problems. Some therapists use a biofeedback apparatus to indicate the suppressed traumas. The beginnings and endings of life do not always come easily. This is an expression of the conflict between soul and the physical plane.

Physical life begins with conception. The constellation of the heavens at conception as well as the inward attitude of your parents during this has a direct correspondence with your soul. An astrological chart depicts your karmic story and what issues you carried over to this life.

Since the soul comes into this world and is incarnated here in order to solve previous situations and to improve itself, it is attracted by parents who have similar interests. This shared motivation is already present at conception. The external circumstances of conception, pregnancy and birth are a reflection of the inner situation of the child.

There has been a great deal of research published on how the mother's experience affects the child in her womb. The true beginning of this analogy, however, is to be found in the child's choice of its parents before conception.

When in the early stages of your regression, the investigation of your birth as well as your prenatal phase is done first. It is learned how your parents felt about your imminent arrival; the way they coped with it, whether or not you were wanted, their fears, their losses, what they expected of you and how they behaved to each other during those long months you remained in the womb. What happened during your actual birth is also explored.

"All the typical benefits and difficulties which we have in our lives as well as many health disorders have their trigger in this prenatal phase and in the birth," says Ingrid.

Reliving what happened before birth often brings out things you never knew before.

These might include family secrets such as the kind Gina discovered about her mother. Perhaps your mother wanted to give you away for adoption or the man you've thought of as a father really isn't that person. If one of your parents died early and you don't remember him or her, you will get to know that person while reliving the pregnancy.

Children sometimes feel guilty when they arrive at a bad time in their parents' lives. They unconsciously promise to make it up to their parents if they'll only love, accept and care for them.

If the mother feels angry and worthless because her husband only married her because she was pregnant, her baby will also feel the same way because it appeared too early and was unwelcome. This will have repercussions in the child's life later.

"When we begin therapy for the prenatal period," explains Ingrid, "I encourage you with such words as 'We are now going into the prenatal phase of the pregnancy. You're already there, in the womb. Give the number of any month from one to nine, whichever comes into your head first.'"

This is the starting point. Now come the first indications and immediately she goes on to ask "if your mother has a problem in this month of her pregnancy, what is it? Tell me word for word what she's thinking this month."

As a rule, she gets immediate answers. Although you're unable to think at that time of your life, your subconscious stores up memories of that period.

What concerns your parents during the pregnancy will concern you in a similar way later in your life.

Ingrid then asks "what difficulties did your mother have during her pregnancy? What worried her? Let your mother say in her own words what she is thinking at such a moment."

She explains that your mother's thoughts and feelings are closer to you than are your father's because she is always with you, while he is only occasionally there.

If one of your parents wants you very much and the other rejects the pregnancy, you may ally yourself with the one who wanted you. You may make promises to this parent such as "I will always help you. I will never be a burden to you. I will protect you and do everything for you."

If there is a question of the pregnancy being rejected, Ingrid looks for promises such as demonstrated here. In later life, this can lead to your having a hard time breaking away from this parent because you don't want to break these promises.

Even when a child is wanted, there may be misgivings regarding the ability of the parents to care properly for their baby. While this is perfectly natural, such ideas can get into a child's subconscious and should be brought to light so as not to have any further influence.

When the prenatal and birth's regression is completed, then is started the regressions into earlier lives.

"We pick up the topic the client wants handled the most. Before any regression into past life is begun, we use such associative questions as: 'If your rash came from a past life, what would be the worst situation happening to your skin? If you knew your current husband from a past life, in which role would you picture him?'" recounts Ingrid.

"Only when the image is clear and contains precise indications that this past life has caused the current stress do we then plunge into regression using phrases like: 'Close your eyes. Now put yourself into that situation just described. Your subconscious will present all the necessary answers. Where are you? What do you see? What do you feel?'"

Since cause and effect and the polarity of issues has to be worked through, one problem area may need two to three regressions before it's complete. The client can then either take a break or express a wish to take up the next topic. In order to handle all major issues of a person, she usually projects ten to twelve regressions. A full therapeutic process of this nature may take about one to two years. Due to the intensity of regressions, the changes that occur are quite profound and may need some time for adjustment to take place.

There are prototypes of past lives that most clients will experience. Since everyone has lived many lives, and since traumas usually affect many people at the same time, everyone has similar experiences. Wars, natural catastrophes and accidents such as shipwrecks affect thousands of people at the same time in a very similar way.

Regressions will uncover such types of incidents as wars, suppression, authoritarian figures, priests and magicians, the Casanova or bon vivant type and victims of natural catastrophes.

In wars, the distress revolves around violence and aggression such as the loss of loved ones, of our possessions and of one's homeland and also insecurity, fear, hunger, injury, and constant threats on one's life, as well as escape and mortal injuries. You may regress to find yourself a foot soldier, cavalryman, sailor, officer, civilian, maid, orphan and victim of violence, rapes or vandalism.

With suppression, are lives lived under the rule of dictators. Under such rulers, the people have often been suppressed and bled with extorting taxes and lack of food staples and being forced into labor. Problems evolve around the fight for survival, hunger, threat, losses, injustice and hatred.

In this type of regression may be found lives as farmers, male and female farm workers or slaves, bondsmen, common soldiers, and mothers losing her children, women losing their husbands, women forced into prostitution, as well as child labor and child abuse, convictions for minor offences, death penalties, death due to inhuman work and exploitation.

Those regressions dealing with authoritarian figures reveal how everyone has, at one time or another played an authoritarian role in ruling over others. It could be as the head of a family clan, a tribe, a landowner, the head of an expedition or an army, as high ranking government officials, aristocrats or religious figures.

Since power is often abused for egotistical purposes, these roles may commit injustices, cruelties, impose unnecessary hardship on their inferiors, and imply greed and vanity and self admiration. Such egomaniac attitudes have often caused the downfall of a group or organism.

Priests and magicians are religious roles that contain the quest for solving the mystery of life. They include self denial, ascetism, hypocrisy, illusion and delusion. If such people exert power over others, they often use hypnosis and manipulation to seduce others to follow them and to comply with their orders. Good potentials and wisdom sometimes have been jeopardized and lost due to vanity, lies and treachery for the sake of material and worldly aims. Sexuality is often abused by religious figures as a means of domination and manipulation.

In this type of regression, you might find yourself to have been a yogi, hermit, herb woman, sorcerer or sorceress, preacher, priest or priestess, monk, nun, shaman, medicine man, black magician or hypnotist.

Opposite of the more serious political roles, you might find yourself remembering a light hearted one where your purpose was to get the most amusement out of life, to play with relationships, laugh off all commitments and deny responsibilities. While it's definitely all right to turn to the bright side of life, problems can arise when you betray other people or reject true love. Then the light heartedness turns to sorrow and regret. In a consequence, the amusing and joyful aspects of life are later condemned.

In such a regression, you might find yourself a vagabond, a Gypsy, Don Juan, seducer, society lady, prostitute, mistress, concubine, musician or artist.

There are many variations of lives that end in natural catastrophes. You might have died as a result of floods, tidal springs, fires, lightning, earthquakes, storms drafts, plagues, or the destruction of a harvest. You might have been injured, caught and imprisoned in fallen debris, become disoriented, lose your family and your own life and all your possessions.

Such traumas are at the root of all commonly known fears such as fear of the future, of loss, of water, of fire, of heights or of sudden interventions. You might feel because of this trauma that your efforts are in vain. This might also cause pain and psychosomatics, since violent deaths cause the body to hurt and be mortally injured. This might manifest itself in this life as asthma, respiratory problems, headaches, back pains or circulatory problems.

You may uncover a former life as a professional engineer, architect, scientist, metal smith, construction worker, herb woman, midwife, doctor, astrologer or magician, for example.

Other people's lives depended on your knowledge. If this judgment was wrong, causing a life being lost, you might have been accused and killed or made to suffer such guilt that your own life became unbearable. Failure in an earlier life will bring about insecurity and fear of responsibility in this life.

Past lives are like archetypes and correspond to the basic colors of a prism. We have lived through all the basic experiences, but the shades of color and their combinations make our personality. Some may pay more attention to one specific area or another, but at the end of a completed past life therapy, all basic issues must be covered and a variety of all major types of past lives should have been regressed. Likes and dislikes lose their intensity, and life is taken at its best for it's in present time. All experiences are equal, and the freedom to choose any venue without karmic repercussions is restored.

CHAPTER 27

INGRID REMEMBERS PAST LIVES

Over the years, Ingrid has been regressed by a number of other people and has regressed herself as well using her own techniques.

As she learned in her own self-explorations, "We all have had female and male lifetimes."

She recalls one lifetime when she was a female and one of a team of cooks for a Chinese empress. This was very weary and tiring. At every meal the Empress wanted to choose from 200 dishes. She would only nibble at a few, and the rest of the food was thrown away. It was stressful to please the empress and you were never far away from being dismissed or punished Needless to say, up through this present lifetime Ingrid doesn't care to cook!. When she has friends over, she often jokes about "having been up all night to cook and prepare the meal." They know it is a joke since Ingrid avoids cooking in any way! Yes, jokes often contain truths about past identities!

She remembers a number lifetimes which she spent as a peasant, a handmaiden, a clerk, a servant. I have found that for many of us, living many lifetimes is very common.

One of her more interesting lifetimes was as the daughter of a merchant on a ship who started in Italy and went to the Orient, buying and selling, exporting and importing spices.

Ingrid recalls it as an exciting life that took her to many foreign countries. In the Orient she had to dress like a man to avoid sexual harassment. Up to her lifetime she has enjoyed bringing specialties as a gift to friends and family from one country to another. Many of her feminine lives are mentioned also earlier.

In her last lifetime she was a German soldier who fought in World War II. In that life, she remembers, she was born in the vicinity of Prague on June 8, 1917.

Growing up in a rural area, Ingrid was the son of farmers. Life on the farm was quite monotonous. Even as in this life, she had adventurous ambitions and a longing to know more of the world.

As the young farmer, she left home at the first opportunity and was recruited into the army at the age of twenty. The army was exciting because in it she got to see things and places she'd only dreamed of before. She got along well with her fellow soldiers.

"We weren't aware that a war was just around the corner, and I took the military exercises as a welcomed change to the farm work at home. I had a deep-felt love for my country and a true loyalty to her ideals. The army was so much more exciting than the previous boring life at home," she remembered during this regression.

"When the war broke out in 1939, it took me all over Germany and then to France. France then seemed a strange land although it looked somehow familiar to me. (In another incarnation I had been a mistress of a French aristocrat.)

"Now, in World War II, I was a foot soldier. Most of the time I walked everywhere. I tramped the fields, the woods, the dirty streets of towns. Sometimes I rode in tanks. I was quite lucky, as I never encountered any severe injury nor did I lose a close friend as long as I was near him.

Until the war's end, she says, she always looked on the conflict as a necessary activity and never regretted her decision to join.

"Of course, I may not have had a chance to decide otherwise after the war broke out," she adds.

In this wartime life she safely returned to Cologne, tired but satisfied, and was transferred to the interior department to do office work which was relaxing after all the stressful journeys and nights spent outside. On the other hand, office work was boring, and she had a lot of time to think over the next few months.

On the inside, she was glad the war was over, and knew this was the time for a new beginning. Her soldier persona had not questioned what the war really was about. In this war-oriented lifetime during World War II, she had tried to be loyal to her country and do as well as she could.

Working in Cologne in the early post war years, it seemed the difficult times had come to an end. The young soldier that she was in this past lifetime was willing to aid the efforts of former enemies working to rebuild the country. But a few other former German soldiers believed he was a traitor who was favoring the conquerors over his own people by being too helpful and friendly. They gunned him down on April 3, 1945.

Ironically the young soldier survived the hardships of war only to die because of the prejudice and misunderstandings of others.

One of Ingrid's best friends in that lifetime was her father in this life, which is why she chose to reincarnate as his child in 1953.

"Even today, vestiges of my most recent past life are apparent in my personality. I love taking long walks and hikes,' she says. "During these walks, I tend to look on the ground a lot as I did in that past life. Then I watched out for traps, hand grenades, land mines or anything else that might harm me; today it's just habit.

"I have always been self disciplined. I was ambitious, whether to be the best I could be in school, in my private education or my professional training. I diligently built up my own practice and institute for seminars and therapy. Martial arts fascinate me, and I took my first classes in it when I was 16, something I continue to do even now."

Since her last life was cut off when she was only 27 years old, just at the brink of moving from one important phase of life to another,

Ingrid says she took a lot of determination with her to this, her next life.

"I was going to make it this time," she says. "I was in a hurry to achieve, to learn and to travel even when I was young, fearful that my life might be cut short again.

"I have no sympathy for 'losers.' You make your own destiny. Even if things get rough, this is only one more challenge to overcome in this lifetime.

"As someone who attended one of my seminars once told me, 'You practice therapy just like a samurai.' If I do, it's a carryover from another of my former lives in which I really was one of those ancient warriors.

"In that lifetime, I was born April 4 in 300 B.C. in Hakodate, Japan. I was 46 years old when I died.

"The son of a governor or viceroy, I was introduced into the ceremonies at an early stage, and I was familiar with government service. Physically, I was well built, and began my samurai training at a very young age.

"When I was 28, I had to past severe tests and examination of my mental concentration as well as my fighting technique and reaction speed. If I hadn't won the test, I would have been chased away to never come back to that town again. I developed an intuition and an extreme perception of my senses, both physically and mentally regarding from where attacks originated. It was as if I had the ability to sense an attacker coming from behind me and be able to counter attack."

Ninja techniques render someone almost invisible because of their swiftness and chameleon ability to disguise themselves and hide from others.

Soon appointed the leader of a fighting squad which was designed to spot adversaries of the Emperor and to annihilate them, she was severe and adamant. Frivolous mistakes, betrayal, passing on of secret information or treason were all punished by death. She fought and killed many adversaries while roaming the land. The respected man she became was honored by the Emperor. Invincible and very fast, she spotted and prevented many conspiracies before they even came to life.

"Women were of minor importance to me," she remembers. "I never married nor had a family. It was very dangerous for women to engage with me, since I was leading a dangerous life.

"I lived in the outskirts of towns, in nature, in the woods. My men roamed and controlled the whole country, and we earned an excellent reputation. After the Emperor retired, I also withdrew and left my work to the others. That winter I became ill with pneumonia and bronchitis. I became weak. Breathing was painful. As I died in a hut in Hokkaido, I thought back about the women I had left behind."

Ingrid remembers that it was a life full of hardship, abstention, concentration on the physical and mental abilities and loyalty. She spent too little time on the well being of others including herself. This would become important in her next life which was that of a Japanese woman who was protected from the outside world. In that life, she was soft, spending her time acquiring skills and knowledge of the arts. She took care of family ties and depended entirely on husband and family in all personal matters.

Ingrid remembers this as a calm life, private and staying in one place, totally opposite in type of her previous time as a proud samurai warrior.

"I suppose these past lives in Japan reflect my early interest in Asia and its culture as well as my devotion to the martial arts," says Ingrid.

When she first visited that country, she found that the soil had a magnetic attraction for her. It was as if she were "home" and not supposed to leave. While there, she totally aligned with the Japanese. There were no culture shocks or misunderstandings. She accepted it all and saya she was, perhaps even biased in the beginning. She could see no flaw in their culture and even spoke Japanese without an accent.

"As a child I always wanted to have black hair and to look Oriental," says Ingrid.

"My boyfriends and lovers were more often Oriental than any other type. I almost married Phayong in Bangkok and then Makoto in Japan. Due to my thirst for knowledge, I never committed to a man until I had completed my search for enlightenment."

Ingrid explains that in her studies, she was attracted to past life therapy because "it's the most condensed way of getting to the root of things without years of therapy talk. It's a tough but clear cut and well directed, goal oriented method of cutting through problems and of broadening awareness. It is the therapy which requires the most sense of responsibility.

"In my work, I use a lot of intuition and I've acquired so much skill doing regressions that I'm almost psychic in finding causes for mishap or those past lives that are key incidents to the current situations. I'm not the type who mothers and pities, but I rather expect a high sense of responsibility, ethics and determination from my clients as well as myself," she adds.

Looking at our history books it may seem that the last few thousand years we were living in a patriarchic society. But what you do not find in history books is the ubiquitous existence of the matriarchies all over the planet, especially on island cultures.

CHAPTER 28

NEW UNDERSTANDINGS

It has been many years now since Ingrid Vallieres began her journey first into self discovery and then into starting her life's work as one of Germany's pioneer past life therapists.

Following the founding in 1979 of her first profession, a translation office, she founded the Institute for Past Life Research. At that point, her career mushroomed in past life therapy work.

Later she founded Creative Management International, (CMI) which is a consulting firm in which she offers leadership conferences and other services. Initially, Ingrid kept her various businesses separate, but today she finds that many of the companies she works with indicate an interest in having what she calls "extraordinary meetings" in which they want to learn more about such things as reincarnation.

Today, talk of reincarnation, past life therapy and similar subjects once considered to be on the fringe has become commonplace. For example, many people have taken up Yoga as an exercise program, something that seemed esoteric just a few years ago. Meditation is now accepted as well.

Ingrid points out that even some of the more hardcore scientists are not now afraid to speak of things that conventional science does not acknowledge. Today's physicists, for example, who have studied the structure of the atom, have come to the realization that the general form that drives the atom cannot be logically explained. They had to admit that some higher power is behind the workings of the physical universe.

Doctors cannot explain why some patients they have deemed terminal will make a miraculous recovery while other such patients do not. Maybe it's because in those patients who live, the soul power has decided to overcome the obstacle and choose life. In some countries people who are known as healers are allowed to come into hospitals and minister to patients, often with excellent results.

Overall, in the 21st Century there is more interaction between the traditional and past life therapies. There is more and more acceptance of alternative approaches in the healing fields.

Still, even by 1980 Ingrid was having great success offering past life therapy sessions and was building a large clientele. One day, late that fall, a journalist attended a class she was giving. Later, he interviewed her for Esotera, Germany's major metaphysical magazine.

The article, published in 1981, was a very positive one. It aroused so much response that soon her agenda was full of clients who had read the article. Around that same time she had completed a contract as translator for a previous employer, so she was able to concentrate on offering therapy classes and growing this aspect of her business.

By 1987, Ingrid's therapy business was thriving. Others brought to her attention that many untrained consultants were offering past life therapy. She was asked to start training others in the manner in which she had been trained. Although she had been reluctant before, she now decided to do it.

By this time, Ingrid says, she had grown weary of doing the past life therapies.

"After having been working at it for eight years. I thought once of quitting entirely but immediately dismissed the idea. What was all that experience of mine for? There was, I thought, a true necessity for having a well grounded training program in my field. I subsequently developed a program and began my work of training therapists to follow the techniques I had learned and used so successfully."

At that first class, she trained four new therapists. It amazed her how much knowledge she had accumulated about the craft. Since those early days in 1988, she has personally trained over 500 therapists around the world. Most of them are from Canada, Germany, Austria and Switzerland.

In 1981, she met an agent of a small publishing company who said after hearing her speak at a seminar in Bavaria that he thought she should write a book. He added that he would be very interested in publishing it and offered her a contract.

Ingrid told him she was no writer, but he promised her that his company would edit what she wrote.

She worked on what would become her first book off and on for years before she finished it. She called it The Practice of Reincarnation Therapy, which became retitled in English as simply Reincarnation Therapy. Although she had no further correspondence from the publisher, it didn't stop her from being determined to finish the book.

"I kept on writing whenever I could get to it. Finally, it was completed. Unfortunately, I finally heard from that publishing company who told me that the man who asked me to write the book was no longer there. Even worse, they were no longer interested in the project and were returning my contract to me," she says.

The journalist who wrote that long ago article about Ingrid had remained in touch with her. Now she asked him to edit her book and get it into shape. He agreed to do so. Not long after that, she found a new publisher.

"This publishing company was so pleased with Reincarnation Therapy that they signed me up to write two more books. Those two remain available only in German. My first book, translated into English, has sold very well, especially in Germany," she says.

Along with her initial book's publication came television and radio interviews. She went on to complete a German video, titled Reincarnation: The Cycle Of Life that premiered in cities across Europe to great success. An English version of it is also on the market. The video has been showed in European movie theaters as well as on television.

She reports that it was strange that she was first so reluctant to do past life therapy and then, later, to write that first book because both turned out so well. She added that to date no one else has put past life therapy into the kind of structure that she has.

"Some therapists in my field are much less structured in their approach. I believe that my own approach to it is logical and easy to grasp. It is a very precise procedure which may be the reason so many corporations are interested in having me give my seminars," she explains.

In the 1990's, she was approached by the Russian Academy of Science in Moscow about her work in past life therapy. Two of the Russian professors at the academy, Alexander Touner and Georgy Sergeov were not only scientists but were interested in various parapsychology subjects such as reincarnation, astrology, numerology, herbs and Tarot.

She worked together with the two of them in giving seminars and lectures not only in Russia but in Germany and other parts of Europe.

"This is very rewarding work, as many of the Russian people have a profound interest in metaphysical topics," she says.

Because of her service with the academy, in 1999 they granted her an honorary professorship in philosophy.

In 2009, she celebrated her 30th business anniversary with a "Remember Atlantis" party in which all attendees were issued an "intergalactic passport" stating their talents, their life's motto and their past lives. It was in adherence to the memory of mystical Atlantis, that legendary island spoken of by Plato which was said to exist somewhere in the Mediterranean Sea.

Ingrid Vallieres has continued to work and grow all her companies into the 21st Century.

Most recently, she expanded her CMI Management Company to work in various countries around the world, most recently Thailand.

Today she has homes in Stuttgart, Switzerland and Bangkok, Thailand. During one visit there, she met Phayong again, the young man she met so many years ago on her first trip to that country. Her tour guide helped her locate her former lover who was delighted to hear from her.

"We talked and agreed that Phayong would call me that night after 8 p.m.," she reports.

Ingrid spent the day sightseeing with her Thai guide. Calling the hotel for messages, she heard that she had a visitor waiting for her.

"I heard that he had been sitting in my hotel lobby since 3 p.m. waiting for me! My guide and I quickly returned to the hotel, I went to my hotel room to freshen up, as I was dusty and sweaty from one full day of sightseeing. In the meantime, my guide kept Payong company.

Finally, we re-united after 40 years and had a drink at the hotel lobby. So that was very pleasurable. His English has deteriorated much since he's retired and does not need to speak English anymore, and I did not realize he was much older than me in those days. In fact, I learned that he is 20 years older than I am. Anyway he accompanied me in Bangkok, we went sightseeing, took walks at the park and just to be together felt very good."

Still beautiful in her sixties, Ingrid believes in exercising daily and following her strict vegetarian diet, although she admits to having a sweet tooth at times. Age has not stopped her boundless energy. She still travels constantly throughout Europe, Asia and the United States on business and regression work.

Throughout the world, more and more therapists such as Ingrid are doing some kind of regression work. Many of the newest methods originate in the United States before being taken up elsewhere in the world. The subject of past lives and other once esoteric subjects are written about in books and shown in the movies.

She points out that there seems to be a growing interest worldwide in regards to such subjects as alternative medicine as well as the idea of reincarnation. There are numerous books and films centering on past lives that can be found in the main stream of today's culture. For example, Kenneth Branagh's film, Dead Again is about a young couple whose present lives reflect an earlier past life. In the hit movie 'Sleepless In Seattle' the remark is made that "you and Annie have met in another life." There is another current television series documenting reincarnation of children called The Ghost Within My Child. She adds that there are many other films with similar viewpoints.

"Today our story is out of the closet and trumpeted around the world," Ingrid says. "My life work continues its path of discovery, inspiration and growth."

She encourages everyone to explore their own lives. As she will tell you, "Remember, you have nothing to fear from having a regression or several into your past lives. The shadows of our past can still affect us in this our present life, but the truth will liberate us. If there is something hidden in a past life it will not rest until we learn the truth. The truth will set you free."

THE END

SUPPLEMENT

Picture gallery from Ingrid

Some other books written
by Ingrid Vallières

Ingrid's parents (1950)   Ingrid as a baby

Maasdam Liner Voyage Rotterdam - New York (1957)

Ingrid's Classmates - Prom (1967)

First Trip to Japan - surroundet by School Children (1972)

With Japanese Friends at Hotspring

At Japanese University for Conservative Martial Arts, Tokyo

With Sikh Master Dr. Mohan Singh (1970)

Speaking at large European Convention (1987)

Lecturing at Swiss Library (1993)

Seminar in Switzerland (2002)

Second Wedding with Captain Mario Zakaria (1991)

At Korea Open Tournament of Taekwon Do in Seoul (2006)

With Pet Cats Snowflake and Valerie

Ingrid - Today's Portrait (2015)

Praxis der Reinkarnationstherapie
Ingrid Vallieres
9. Auflage,
Das Standardwerk. 256 S.,
Format 20,9 x,14,8 cm, PB,
Print: ISBN 978-3-89594-978-4
PDF: ISBN 978-3-89594-955-5
eBook: ISBN 978-3-89594-968-5

English Version:
Reincarnation Therapy
Print: 978-3-89594-946-3
optional
PDF: 978-3-89594-947-0
eBook: 978-3-89594-948-7

Astrologie und Reinkarnation
I.Vallieres/K.H.Dotter

2. Auflage,
Format 21 x 14,8 cm 152 S., PB,
Print: ISBN 978-3-89594-991-3
PDF: ISBN 978-3-89594-953-1
eBook: ISBN 978-3-89594-954-8

Reinkarnation für Katzen
Ingrid Vallieres
Humorvoll, mit zahlreichen
farbigen Zeichnungen.
Ideal als Geschenk.
Format 13 x 19 cm, 54 S., PB,
Print: ISBN 978-3-89594-994-4
PDF: ISBN 978-3-89594-956-2
eBook: ISBN 978-3-89594-957-9

English Version (available shortly)
Reincarnation for Cats
Print: 978-3-89594-943-2
optional
PDF: 978-3-89594- 944-9
eBook: 978-3-89594-945-6

Schicksalstherapie
Ingrid Vallieres
Spektakuläre Fälle aus der
Reinkarnationstherapie,
kann der Mensch sein Schicksal
beeinflussen?
192 Seiten,
Format 21 x 14,8 cm,
Print: ISBN 978-3-89594-975-3
PDF: ISBN 978-3-89594-949-4
eBook: ISBN 978-3-89594-950-0

Probleme - Nein danke!
I.Vallieres & R.Kiprowski
So bekommen Sie Ihre Probleme in den Griff.
Entdecken Sie Ihr Potential!
120 S., geb.,
Print ISBN 978-3-89594-976-0
PDF: ISBN 978-3-89594-951-7
eBook: ISBN 978-3-89594-952-4